WALLS AND CEILINGS

Other Publications:

FIX IT YOURSELF
FITNESS, HEALTH & NUTRITION
SUCCESSFUL PARENTING
HEALTHY HOME COOKING
UNDERSTANDING COMPUTERS
LIBRARY OF NATIONS
THE ENCHANTED WORLD
THE KODAK LIBRARY OF CREATIVE PHOTOGRAPHY
GREAT MEALS IN MINUTES
THE CIVIL WAR
PLANET EARTH
COLLECTOR'S LIBRARY OF THE CIVIL WAR
THE EPIC OF FLIGHT
THE GOOD COOK
WORLD WAR II
THE OLD WEST

This volume is part of a series offering homeowners
detailed instructions on repairs, construction
and improvements they can undertake themselves.

HOME REPAIR
AND IMPROVEMENT

WALLS AND CEILINGS

BY THE EDITORS OF
TIME-LIFE BOOKS

TIME-LIFE BOOKS
ALEXANDRIA, VIRGINIA

HOME REPAIR AND IMPROVEMENT

Editorial Staff for Walls and Ceilings

Editor	Robert M. Jones
Assistant Editors	Betsy Frankel, Brooke Stoddard
Designer	Edward Frank
Chief Researcher	Oobie Gleysteen
Picture Editor	Neil Kagan
Associate Designer	Kenneth E. Hancock
Text Editors	Leslie Marshall, Katherine Miller
Staff Writers	Lynn R. Addison, Patricia C. Bangs, William C. Banks, Megan Barnett, Michael Blumenthal, Robert A. Doyle, Steven J. Forbis, Bonnie Bohling Kreitler, Victoria W. Monks, Peter Pocock, William Worsley
Art Associates	George Bell, Fred Holz, Lorraine D. Rivard
Copy Coordinator	Margery duMond
Picture Coordinator	Anne Muñoz-Furlong
Editorial Assistant	Susan Larson

Editorial Operations

Copy Chief	Diane Ullius
Editorial Operations Manager	Caroline A. Boubin
Production	Celia Beattie
Quality Control	James J. Cox (director)
Library	Louise D. Forstall

Correspondents: Elisabeth Kraemer-Singh (Bonn); Maria Vincenza Aloisi (Paris); Ann Natanson (Rome). Valuable assistance was also provided by: Judy Aspinall (London); Carolyn T. Chubet, Miriam Hsia, Christina Lieberman (New York); Mimi Murphy (Rome).

THE CONSULTANTS: Gregory Green, a graduate of Brown University, the Rhode Island School of Design and the U.S. Army School of Engineering, is an experienced designer and builder of residential, commercial, hospital and industrial facilities. Throughout his career he has specialized in custom construction of homes and interiors, and in the reconstruction of historic single-family residences.

Claxton Walker, who was a home builder and remodeler for many years in Maryland, Virginia and the District of Columbia, inspects homes for prospective buyers. A former industrial-arts teacher, he lectures at local colleges and before the public on topics including house structure and construction.

Roswell W. Ard is a consulting structural engineer and a professional home inspector in northern Michigan. He has written professional papers on wood-frame construction techniques.

Harris Mitchell, a special consultant for Canada, has worked in the field of home repair and improvement since 1952. He writes a syndicated newspaper column, "You Wanted to Know," and is the author of a number of books on home improvement.

For information about any Time-Life book, please write:
Reader Information
Time-Life Books
541 North Fairbanks Court
Chicago, Illinois 60611

Library of Congress Cataloguing in Publication Data
Time-Life Books.
　　Walls and ceilings.
　　(Home repair and improvement; 22)
　　Includes index.
　　1. Interior walls.　2. Ceilings.　3. Dwellings—
　　Remodeling.　I. Title
TH2239.T55　　1980　　643'.7　　80-13045
ISBN 0-8094-3452-0
ISBN 0-8094-3451-2 (lib. bdg.)
ISBN 0-8094-3450-4 (retail ed.)

Contents

Guardians of Privacy and Comfort

1

A recipe for walls and ceilings. Paper tape, a panful of joint compound—with its wide-spreading knife—and a backdrop of gypsum wallboard represent the three main ingredients for finishing most modern walls and ceilings. The wallboard is fastened with nails or screws to studs or joists, furring strips, or sound-absorbing resilient channels. Then the narrow gaps between the sections of wallboard are filled with joint compound and strengthened with tape and additional thin layers of the compound.

The walls and ceilings of a typical house are its single most extensive feature, presenting a surface measured in thousands of square feet and occupying an area roughly four times that of the floor. Yet, when they are doing their job well, walls and ceilings go almost unnoticed—a backdrop for furniture, lighting and decorative arts.

Despite this seeming unimportance, walls and ceilings perform a variety of valuable functions. They mask the structure and working parts of the house—the studs, joists and rafters, wires and pipes. They reduce the transmission of noise and control the passage of light from one floor to another and from one room to another. And they help to contain damage in the event of fire.

To serve these needs, the basic building material for walls and ceilings must be heavy, easy to work with, fire-resistant and plentiful enough to be inexpensive. The ideal material, discovered by the ancients and tested by thousands of years of use, is gypsum, a relative of common chalk. If you are indoors, you probably are surrounded by gypsum, in the form of either gypsum wallboard or plaster. Even if your room has luxurious wood paneling or expensive hand-painted tile, there probably is a protective layer of wallboard or plaster hidden beneath it.

To create this chalky environment, a staggering amount of gypsum is dug from mines and quarries annually. In the United States and Canada in a recent year, enough gypsum was exhumed to make roughly 20 billion square feet of wallboard and plaster surfaces. Fortunately, the material is plentiful. The known reserves of gypsum pure enough for plaster will last thousands of years. Besides being abundant, gypsum is easily refined into a powder for plaster or formed into sheets of wallboard. Both are sound-absorbing; with special installation techniques, they can provide a virtually soundproof wall or ceiling. Like most other minerals, gypsum is noncombustible. In addition, it possesses an almost miraculous fire resistance; when exposed to fire, gypsum absorbs heat and exudes steam because it is 20 per cent water; when it is heated, the water vapor that is released drives flames away. This phenomenon keeps the temperature on the side of the wall not exposed to flame near 212° for an extended (and potentially life-saving) period.

In use, both wallboard and plaster produce a smooth surface that is an ideal base for paint, wallpaper, tile (ceramic, acoustic or cork) and wood paneling. Wallboard can be used also as a base for a thin veneer of plaster, to combine the durability of plaster with the construction ease of wallboard. And some wallboard manufactured for commercial use is factory-decorated with vinyl wallpaper, making possible a one-step finished wall.

Wall and Ceiling Structures from the Inside Out

The composition of interior walls and ceilings was once quite simple. In log cabins particularly, an interior wall was often just the back of the exterior wall: stacked logs with chinking between them. In like manner the ceiling often consisted of beams, rafters and the underside of the roof.

But as building technology advanced, the inside and outside of a wall or ceiling became separate entities. With the development of the circular mill saw and mass-produced nails, the construction of wood houses evolved from a simple configuration of heavy timbers to an intricate framework of much lighter but more numerous components, into whose skeletal structure were fitted such necessities of modern life as plumbing, electrical wiring and insulation. An understanding of the nature of this construction is essential to much of the work discussed in this book.

In the United States and Canada, wood is the material most commonly used for the framework of a house. The walls of these wood-frame houses consist of vertical members, called studs, and horizontal members, the top plates and sole plates. All of these are usually cut from 2-by-4 stock, although in recent years some builders have switched to 2-by-6s to give space for a greater thickness of insulating material. Larger boards called joists—generally at least 2-by-8s—are set horizontally and on edge to define every ceiling. These ceiling joists also support the floor of any living space overhead; hence the terms "ceiling joist" and "floor joist" are often used interchangeably.

The alternative to wood framing is masonry construction. The inside of the exterior walls of masonry houses—especially older ones—often consists of plaster laid on brick, but most such houses have ceilings and partition walls framed with wood joists and studs. Studs also lie behind the brick exteriors of many modern houses that are actually brick veneer, in which a single layer of brick has been added to the outside of standard wood-framed walls.

A wall that supports the roof or other upper structural parts of a house is known as a bearing (or sometimes load-bearing) wall, and this important role influences its composition. In masonry houses, interior bearing walls are usually of masonry construction. Bearing walls in many frame houses are strengthened by the placement of the studs at closer intervals. Ceiling joists run perpendicular to bearing walls, and there are a variety of techniques (box, below) for determining both stud and joist placement—information that is essential for almost any job on a wall or ceiling.

Wall coverings also vary according to the construction and age of a house. In homes built before 1950, plaster over a bonding surface known as lath was the most common wall surface. Originally the lath consisted of short wood strips, but wood lath became obsolete in the 1930s and was replaced first by wire lath and then by gypsum lath (page 26).

Soon after World War II, gypsum wallboard replaced plaster as a finish surface in most new construction because it is more easily and quickly installed. Wallboard, unlike plaster, requires no drying time and it comes in 4-by-8-, 4-by-10- or 4-by-12-foot panels that cover large areas quickly without the intermediary lath. The panels were once installed vertically, but now they are usually positioned horizontally on a wall because this reduces the number of joints to be concealed.

The pictures on the following two pages illustrate some of the typical combinations of structural anatomy and finish surfaces found in wall and ceiling construction. Some details, such as the insulation that would be found between the studs of exterior frame walls, have been omitted, in order to increase the clarity of the drawings.

Locating Concealed Studs and Joists

For most work on walls and ceilings, it is necessary to determine the positions of concealed studs and joists, and there are several techniques for doing so. You can tap lightly along the wall or ceiling until you hear a solid sound, which usually indicates a stud or joist, then move over 16 inches—the most common distance between framing members—and tap again. It is also possible to locate structural supports by driving finishing nails into the wall or ceiling at several points until they meet resistance.

To confirm the spacing indicated by either technique, drill a small hole in an inconspicuous spot and probe behind the surface with a stiff wire (right); when the wire hits a joist or stud, place a finger on the wire where it enters the hole, to record the distance to the stud.

If the repair work makes it necessary for you to remove a baseboard, it is usually easy to check behind the baseboard for visible seams or nails where the wallboard panels cross a stud. You can also examine a ceiling close up, standing on a chair or ladder, for traces of tape seams or nailing patterns along the joists; this is best done at night with an overhead light on.

Many hardware stores sell a simple device, called a stud finder, containing a magnet that reacts to the nails driven into studs or joists. Many such magnets are weak, however, so the device is most useful if the nails are fairly large and near the surface of the wall.

Once you have located one stud or joist—by whatever technique—you will be able to mark its path along the ceiling or wall simply by measuring out an equivalent distance elsewhere on the surface. Then snap a chalk line between the two points.

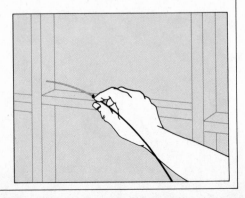

Surfaced Wood-Frame Walls

Wallboard over studs and joists. On this modern wood-frame wall, 4-by-8 panels of wallboard are secured horizontally with nails and an adhesive to vertical 2-by-4 studs. The studs are nailed on edge between the sole plate (a horizontal 2-by-4 at floor level) and the top plate (doubled horizontal 2-by-4s at ceiling level). The studs are spaced at 16-inch intervals, center to center. Firestops—short 2-by-4s nailed horizontally between studs at staggered levels—retard the spread of flames if fire breaks out.

Studs are doubled alongside door and window openings and a heavy beamlike assembly called a header extends above each opening. Short stud sections, known as trimmer studs or cripple studs, extend above each header as well as below the rough sill, a 2-by-4 that runs across the bottom of each window opening.

On the ceiling, wallboard is attached to 2-by-10 joists that are spaced at 16-inch intervals. The joists rest on, and are toenailed to, the top plates of two bearing walls.

Most plumbing pipes that run vertically through a wall pass through holes drilled in the sole and top plates; pipes that must run perpendicular to studs or joists are fitted into notches cut in the edges of these members. Vertical runs of electrical cable are stapled to the sides of the studs or joists; horizontal cables are threaded through ¾-inch holes in studs or joists.

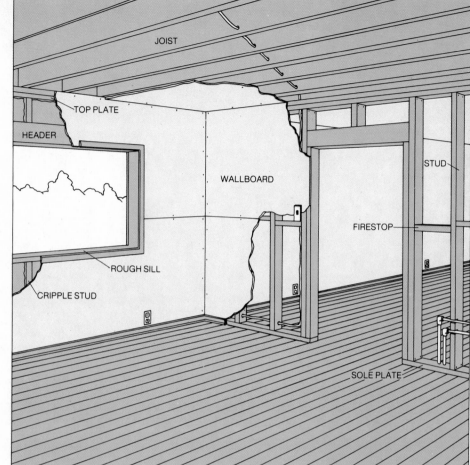

Plaster over wood lath. The plaster finish over a busy pattern of wood strips, called wood lath, that covers this wood-framed wall and ceiling is typical of house construction prior to 1930. The structural anatomy of the stud walls and ceiling joists here is identical to modern frame construction (*above*), except that the spacing between the older members varies from 12 to 24 inches. The wood strips—generally ⁵⁄₁₆ inch thick, 1½ inches wide and long enough to span three or four studs—are nailed to the studs and joists in staggered groups of four to six.

The ¼-inch gaps between wood strips allow the plaster, which is applied in two or three coats, to ooze through the lath to anchor itself. At the corners of the room the wood lath is strengthened with a 4- to 6-inch-wide strip of metal lath, bent to fit and nailed in place.

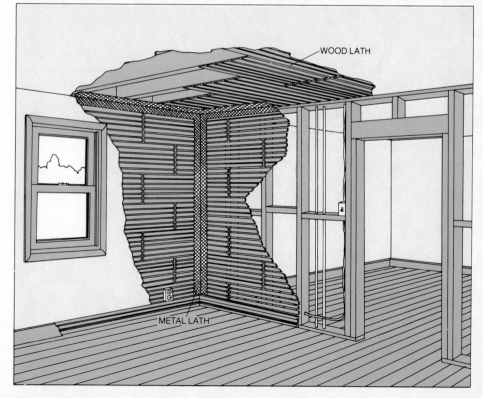

Finished Surfaces over Masonry Walls

Wallboard attached to furring strips. On this concrete-block wall, wallboard is nailed to vertical 1-by-3 wood strips, called furring strips, that are spaced at 16-inch intervals and secured to the blocks with either masonry nails, adhesive or a combination of the two. Miniature stud walls of 2-by-3s or 2-by-4s enclose any exposed pipes. Overhead, wallboard is attached to 2-by-10 ceiling joists whose ends rest in pockets made in the masonry walls at the time of construction.

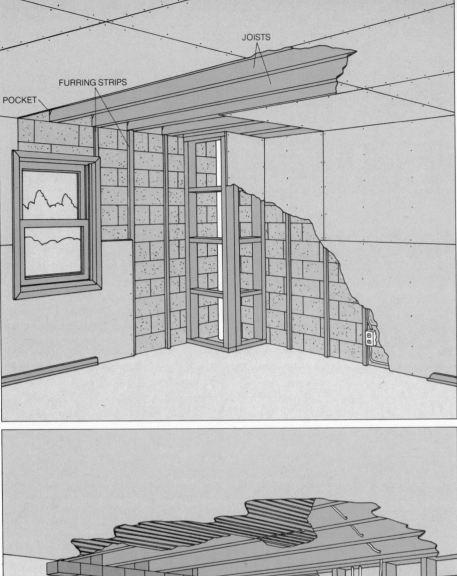

Plaster-over-masonry walls. In this masonry house typical of the early 1900s, all exterior walls as well as interior bearing walls consist of two layers of brick separated by an air space of about 2 inches and reinforced with metal ties. Non-bearing interior walls, such as the one on the right in this drawing, are framed with wood studs.

The plaster finish on the interior masonry walls is applied directly to the bricks; on the stud walls and ceiling joists the base underlying the plaster is wood lath. Metal lath reinforces the corners where the two walls meet. The ends of the ceiling joists rest in pockets that were made in the brick walls at the time of construction.

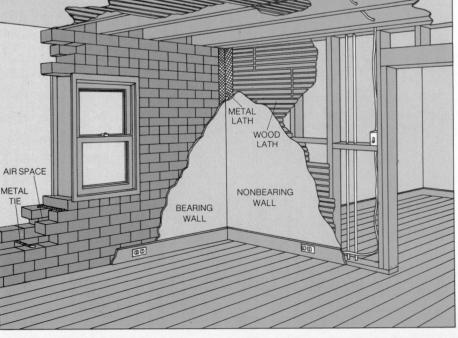

Truing Up Hills and Valleys for Resurfacing

The key to a smooth wall or ceiling is a flat, sound substructure for the surface material. While some walls are sound enough to be resurfaced directly, others need extensive preparation to compensate for surface damage or crooked framing members. You may have to make a grid of thin wood furring strips to serve as a flat base. You may even have to build a false wall in front of the old one.

To assess the condition of an uneven wall or ceiling, you will need a carpenter's level and a long straight-edged board. First hold the level against the wall at several places to check it for plumb, or against the ceiling to check that it is level. Then slide the board across the wall or ceiling as you look for gaps between board and surface. If neither check discloses major flaws, you can probably install the new surface over the old with only minor preparations. If you plan to use adhesive, make sure the old surface is clean; if the new surface will be fastened to the old framing, mark the positions of the wall studs or ceiling joists.

On surfaces where only small areas are damaged or out of true, you can use plywood or wallboard patches to repair the damage, shimming the patches to bring them flush with the surrounding surface. When the surface is badly damaged,

however, or very uneven, you will have to build out the entire wall or ceiling with a grid of furring strips, shimming them as necessary to produce a level base. For the shims, use cedar shingles, making the required thickness by sliding two shingles together with their thin ends in opposite directions.

Sometimes, if the existing surface is basically true, you can check by eye alone to see if the shimmed furring strips are true. But you may need to rule off the wall or ceiling with reference lines and strings and take careful measurements, to level the grid. On the sound sections of wall or ceiling around your working area, use erasable pencil or chalk.

In laying out a furring grid, you will have to deal with interruptions in the surface. Remove moldings and trim, and adjust the depth of door and window jambs to suit the new wall thickness. You may have to reposition electrical outlet boxes, or adjust their depth.

The pattern for the grid may require some preliminary thought. Although furring strips usually run horizontally, some materials, such as plywood paneling, require vertical supports as well, and you must plan the layout of the panels in advance, so that the vertical supports match the panel edges.

Furring out from a masonry wall presents other problems. You must use case-hardened cut nails, or use cut nails and construction adhesive. On any masonry wall below ground level, you must put a moisture barrier of vinyl sheeting before attaching the furring strips.

If the watertightness of the masonry might be impared by nails driven into it, you may have to erect a false wall of 2-by-3 or 2-by-4 studs in front of the real wall. A false wall may also be needed for the junction boxes or switches for a new electric circuit, since junction-box holes could create leaks in the masonry and even violate local fire codes.

Sometimes built-ins or plumbing fixtures make it impossible to fur out a wall or build a false one. Sometimes, too, a surface will be too badly damaged to serve as the base for a new one—plaster may be too loose or wallboard too crumbly. In such cases you will have to remove the existing wall surface and start from scratch, laying the resurfacing material directly against the framing studs. Although this sounds drastic, it is not hard. Wallboard can generally be pulled off, or plaster broken, with a hammer, after which the lath can be pried out with a utility bar. Before installing the new surfacing material, sink any protruding nails.

A Gridiron Pattern for Furring Strips

A framework for plywood paneling. The furring strips on this wall, backed by thin wood shims where needed, make a flat, plumb base for vertical 4-foot-by-8-foot plywood panels. The horizontal strips are 1-by-2s, spaced 16 inches apart from center to center. Vertical furring strips, also 1-by-2s, are placed across the wall at 48-inch intervals, center to center.

Small gaps between vertical and horizontal furring strips prevent moisture damage by letting air circulate behind the paneling. Additional 1-by-2s frame the corners and window to support the panel edges, and a furring strip that spans two studs will support an electrical outlet. The horizontal 1-by-4 furring strips at the top and bottom of the wall serve as the backing for the crown and base moldings that will be nailed to the wall after the paneling is in place.

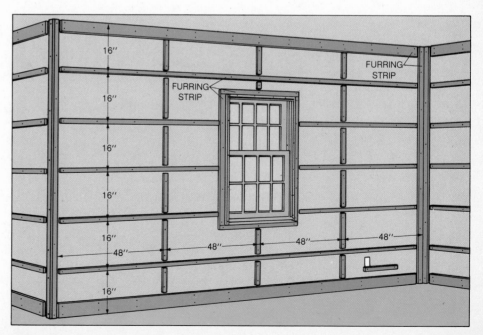

FURRING STRIP

FURRING STRIP

Prying Off Molding and Trim

1 Removing a length of molding. To salvage a length of shoe molding, first cut through the paint at the seam between the molding and the baseboard with a utility knife, then drive a thin pry bar into the seam near an end of the molding. Place a wooden block behind the pry bar to protect the baseboard, and slowly pry the molding loose. Work along the seam, using wedges to hold the seam open as you go, until the whole length of molding is loose enough to remove in one piece. Use the same technique to remove baseboards and other moldings.

2 Removing window or door trim. To avoid splitting window or door casings as you pry them loose, use a nail set to drive the existing nails completely through one section of each mitered corner. Then you will be able to pry off the casing, using the technique described in Step 1, left.

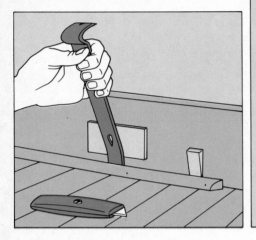

Guidelines and Shims to Position Furring

1 Setting up reference lines. With a pencil and straightedge, rule off the wall (*top right*) with a gridwork of lines marking the vertical locations of framing studs in the wall and horizontal positions where furring strips will be installed. Then snap a chalk line against the ceiling, 2 inches out from the wall.

On a ceiling (*bottom right*), mark two reference lines by first marking the location of concealed joists, then snapping a chalk line along each of the two walls that parallel the joists. Place these chalk lines about 2 inches below ceiling level. Drive nails along each chalk line at the position for furring strips, and run taut strings across the joists between opposing nails.

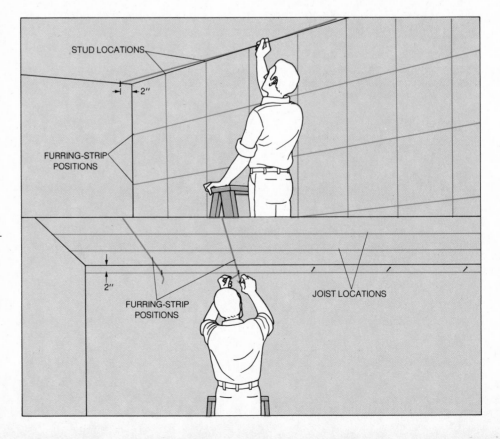

2 **Positioning the first furring strips.** Suspend a plumb bob from the ceiling chalk line (2 inches from the wall) so that it hangs in front of a wall stud, and measure the distance from the plumb line to the wall at each intersection of stud and furring-strip line. Record each measurement. Repeat at the other studs.

When you have found the point with the smallest measurement—the highest point along the wall—nail a horizontal furring strip with a single nail to the wall at this point. Position the plumb bob in front of this point and note the distance from the plumb line to the face of the furring strip. In positioning the strip, leave room at the corner for a vertical furring strip. When several points along the wall are the same short distance from the plumb line, nail a furring strip to the wall with a single nail at each such point.

Use the same procedure to locate the lowest point on the ceiling, measuring from the intersections of the strings to the ceiling. At the lowest point, slip a furring strip under the strings and nail it with a single nail to a joist. Measure and make a note of the distance between the string and the furring strip at this point.

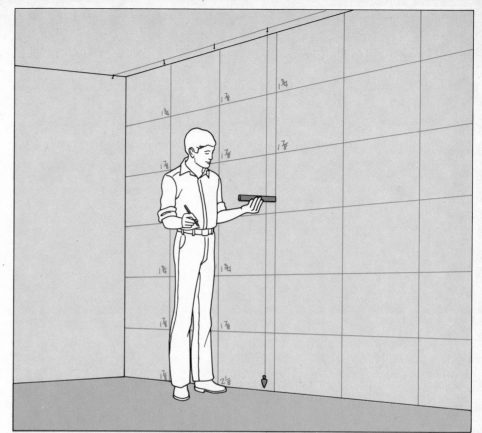

3 **Shimming the first furring strip.** Reposition the plumb bob, hanging it from the ceiling chalk line in front of the stud nearest one end of the furring strip. Place wood shims as necessary behind the strip until the distance between its face and the plumb line measures the same as the distance at the first nailing point. Drive a nail through the furring strip and the shims and into that stud. Position the other end of the furring strip in the same way.

On a ceiling, shim out one end of the furring strip until the distance from the string to the face of the furring strip is the same as at the first nailing point. Nail the strip to the joist nearest the end of the strip. Then repeat at the opposite end.

4 Truing a furring strip. Press the edge of a long straight board against the first furring strip, spanning two nailed points, and note where the furring strip, when pressed against the wall, bows away from the straight edge. Build these points out with shims at each stud as you nail the furring strip in place.

Repeat Steps 3 and 4 to install a second furring strip at the top or bottom of the wall, adjusting it with shims so it is set the same distance from the plumb line as the first strip. On a ceiling, use the same technique to true and nail the first furring strip, then install and true a second strip at one side, setting it the same distance from the reference strings as the first strip.

5 Installing the remaining furring. Hold the edge of the long straight board vertically, spanning the two trued furring strips, and use it as a reference for installing and shimming the rest of the horizontal strips in the grid. Then install vertical strips where they are needed, shimming them to lie flush with the horizontal strips. At corners, install full-length vertical strips; at mid-wall, cut them to fit between the horizontal strips. Short vertical strips need not be fastened to studs; they can be secured to the old wall with adhesive or nails.

Use the same techniques to install the remaining furring strips on a ceiling. Then add short cross strips where needed to support panel edges.

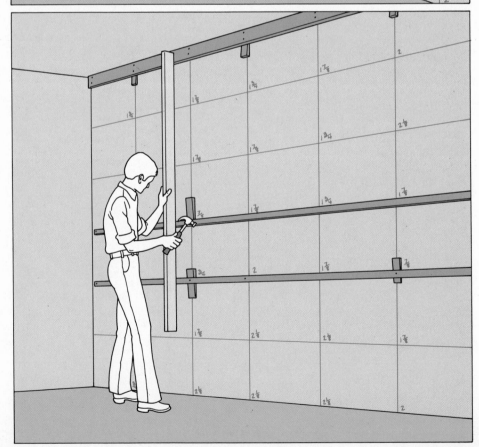

A False Wall over Masonry

1 Making the frame. For the top and sole plates of a false wall, cut two 2-by-4s the length of the planned wall, and lay them on the floor, face up and side-by-side, with their ends aligned. With a framing square and pencil, mark the stud positions across both plates simultaneously. Mark the first stud position flush with one end of the plates. Place the center of the second stud position 16 inches in from the end of the plate, and mark for the centers of subsequent studs at 16-inch intervals. But make the last stud flush with the opposite end of the plates, no matter how close it is to the next-to-last stud.

Turn the plates on edge, the marked faces toward each other, and position 2-by-4 studs, cut 3½ inches shorter than the ceiling height. Fasten each stud with two 10-penny nails driven through the plate and into the stud, top and bottom.

2 Erecting the framing. With a helper, raise the wall framing into position and hold a carpenter's level against the studs at several points to make sure the framing is plumb. Shim between the top plate and the finished ceiling or exposed joists for a tight fit. Then nail the side and top plates to the floor and the ceiling with 16-penny nails (or, if the floor is concrete, use case-hardened cut nails).

Nail horizontal 2-by-4s (*inset*) between studs at 24-inch intervals to provide additional support for the panels that will be mounted vertically. Install similar blocks to serve as nailing surfaces around electric outlet boxes or to support doors that will later be cut in the paneling to provide access to plumbing (*page 75*).

Enclosures to Conceal Pipes and Ducts

Framing with miniature stud walls. Most pipes, ducts and girders can be enclosed with smaller, three-dimensional versions of the false stud wall. A vertical enclosure (*below, left*) is made of two narrow vertical walls reinforced with horizontal supports, called blocking. The top plate of one wall is nailed to a ceiling joist, and the top plate of the other is nailed to a 2-by-4 between joists. Adjoining end studs of the two walls are nailed together at the corner; the bottom plates of each wall are nailed to the floor.

A horizontal enclosure (*below, right*) consists of two stud-wall assemblies with very short studs; one assembly is constructed vertically and the other horizontally. The adjoining plates of the two sections are nailed together at the outside corner; the opposite plate of the horizontal frame is nailed to wall studs, while the top plate of the vertical frame is nailed to ceiling joists—or, if necessary, to horizontal blocking that has been installed between joists.

For three-sided enclosures, either horizontal or vertical, first construct and install two stud walls for the parallel sides of the enclosure. Then install blocking to form the third side.

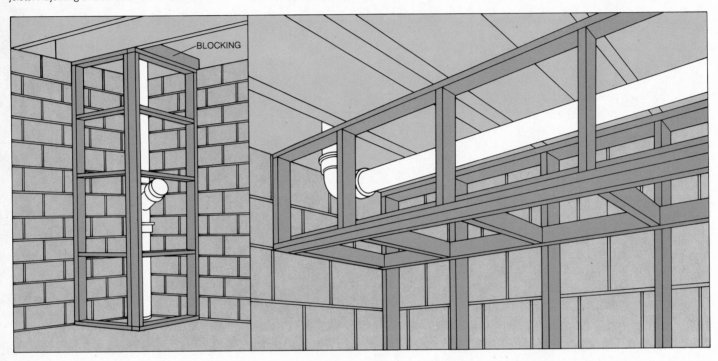

BLOCKING

Widening the Window Jambs

1 Removing a window stool. If you plan to extend a window jamb that has a window stool (inner sill) at the bottom, first pry off the window's interior stops, using the technique on page 12. Then drive all of the existing nails through the horn of the stool into the jamb as in Step 2, page 12. Pry up the stool and use it as a pattern for cutting a new stool (*inset*), extending the back edge of the stool to match the extended jamb. Generally the increase in this dimension will be equal to the thickness of the furring strips plus the thickness of the new wall surface.

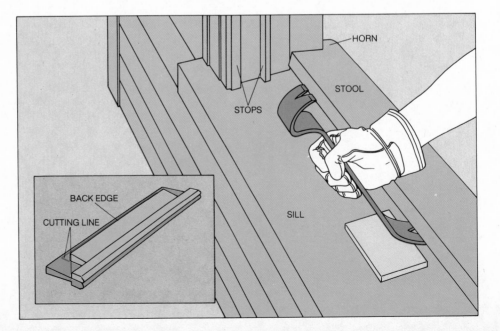

HORN

STOOL

STOPS

SILL

BACK EDGE

CUTTING LINE

2 **Attaching jamb extensions.** From ¾-inch-thick stock, cut three jamb extensions—two for the sides, one for the top. The width of the extensions should equal the combined thickness of the furring strips and the new wall surface. Nail the extensions to the edges of the existing jambs with finishing nails.

If paneling has been applied directly to an existing wall, without furring, extend the jamb with ¼-by-¾-inch lattice. By using thinner stock, you avoid the tricky job of cutting a long thin strip from a wider board.

Extending an Electric Outlet Box

Attaching a box extender. Cut off the electricity at the fuse box, take off the faceplate of the electric outlet or switch, and remove the screws that secure the fixture, top and bottom, to its metal box. Slide a collar-like extender over the fixture and its wiring and into the box. Use the long bolts that are supplied with the extender to reattach the fixture to the box, adjusting the position of the extender so that the fixture will lie flush with the new wall surface.

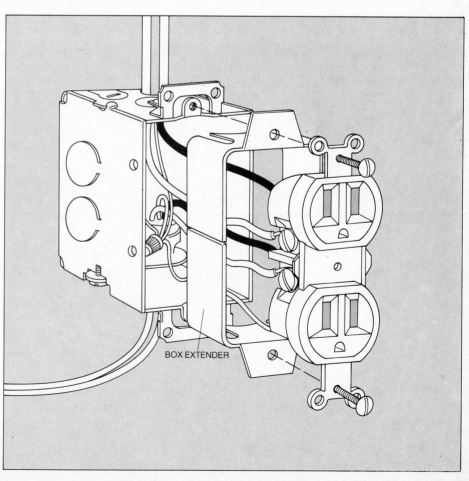

BOX EXTENDER

Finished Surfaces in a Hurry with Wallboard

Wallboard, the material most commonly used to finish walls and ceilings, is simply a sheet of chalklike gypsum between two layers of heavy paper. The gypsum core is softened with additives, chiefly ground-up newspapers, that make the board easy to cut and somewhat flexible.

Wallboard can be fastened by a variety of means—nails, screws, adhesives—to a variety of supporting structures: joists, furring strips or studs of wood or metal. The joints where panels meet are concealed with a special adhesive tape or with a paper tape embedded in several layers of doughlike joint compound.

Reflecting its varied applications, wallboard comes in several forms. One is made for bathrooms and has a high degree of water resistance. Another, called Type X, is especially resistant to fire and is specified by some local codes for fire-prone areas such as garages. Generally made in 4-foot widths, wallboard comes in 8-, 10- and 12-foot lengths and in thicknesses of ⅜, ½ and ⅝ inch; ½-inch wallboard is considered standard.

Using 12-foot boards will save time, reducing the number of joints to be finished. But such boards are heavy and unwieldy. Two professionals can lift and install a ½-inch wallboard ceiling panel 12 feet long, but you may need three people—and even then the job may be daunting. If so, install shorter boards. In either case simplify the finishing of end joints by creating a recess, using a technique called back-blocking *(page 20)*.

Next, to find how many boards you will need, calculate the square footage of each wall, ignoring all openings except the largest, such as archways or picture windows. Do the same for the ceiling. Then translate this figure into boards; an 8-foot wallboard contains 32 square feet, and a 12-foot wallboard 48 square feet.

You will also need fasteners. When the underpinnings are wood, as is usually the case, nails are the most-used fasteners, although nails may eventually pop away from the surface of the board if the wood is green. To avoid this problem, you can use special dry-wall screws made for walls framed with metal studs *(page 62)*. These have Phillips heads and can be driven quickly with an electric screw gun or a variable-speed electric drill fitted with a Phillips bit. Whether you use screws or nails, you will also need wallboard adhesive. Its use cuts down the number of screws or nails required and greatly increases strength.

With materials in hand, you are ready to begin. Construct the ceiling first, then the walls, always beginning in a corner. Measure and cut the boards so that end-to-end joints fall at joists or studs (except in back-blocking) and are staggered by at least 16 inches in adjacent rows. Space nails and screws at recommended intervals and omit fasteners entirely within 8 inches of a corner in order to create floating joints that are less likely to crack if the house settles.

Professionals prefer to install wallboard panels horizontally, rather than vertically, on walls. Usually the result is a wall with fewer joints and fewer dips and bows; boards used horizontally tend to bridge studs that are out of line. Wherever possible, place boards so that joints fall along the frames of doors and windows, thus making fewer joints to seal.

When you install wallboard horizontally, you may need a filler strip to bring the wall to ceiling height. Most professionals put this strip in the center of the wall, between the two 4-foot boards, and cover the two joints with one wide swath of joint compound. But it takes skill to make these joints smooth since at least one of them is bound to involve a nontapered edge. You can avoid this problem if you put the filler strip at the bottom of the wall, cut edge down. The finishing process is simpler, and the bottom joint may be hidden by the baseboard.

One final word about exterior walls: Before you install wallboard, make sure you have sufficient insulation. If necessary, add insulating batts, with the vapor barrier facing into the room, fastening them to the sides of the wall studs.

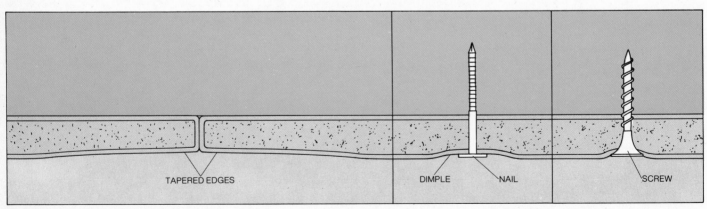

TAPERED EDGES   DIMPLE   NAIL   SCREW

A wallboard cross section. Wallboard consists of a gypsum core covered front and back with heavy paper. The long edges of the panel are slightly tapered *(above, left)* starting 2 inches from the edge, so that when two boards are butted together, they form a shallow trough, simplifying the job of covering the joint.

Special dry-wall nails, which are often made with ringed shafts for extra grip *(above, middle)*, can be used to fasten the wallboards to wooden framing members or to furring strips. The nails are driven until their heads are slightly below the surrounding paper surface, leaving a hammer-made dimple that is later filled with joint com-

pound. Neither the nailhead nor the dimple should break the paper surface.

Screws *(above, right)* can be used with either metal or wood framing structures. The screws should be sunk to just below the wallboard surface, leaving the paper intact.

Fitting Boards as a Pro Does

Shortening a panel. Hold a straightedge or the long arm of a wallboard T square perpendicular to the side of the board and cut through the paper surface with a utility knife. Grasp the edge of the board on both sides of the cut line and snap the short section of board away from you, breaking the gypsum along the scored line. With the short section cocked back slightly, reach behind the board and, with the utility knife, make a foot-long slit in the paper along the bend. Then swing the short section forward to split the paper and separate the section.

Making openings. To mark a board for a small opening such as the hole for an electrical outlet or switch box, use a professional's trick with a steel tape and pencil. Measure across from the point where the side edge of the board will rest to the near and far sides of the installed box. Similarly, measure from the point where the top or the bottom edge of the board will fall (whichever is closer) to the top and bottom of the box.

To transfer these measurements to the board (not yet installed), grasp the measuring tape between the thumb and forefinger of one hand so that a length of tape corresponding to the first measurement projects beyond your thumbnail. Rest the side of your forefinger against the appropriate edge of the board and hold a pencil against the end of the tape with the other hand. Move both hands down the board simultaneously, keeping them parallel, to mark the first of the four edges of the opening. Repeat with each of the other three measurements. Cut the opening with a wallboard saw (*page 22*) or a keyhole saw. For a larger opening, such as a window, mark the wallboard in the same way. Cut all four sides with a saw or, if you wish, saw three sides, then score and break the fourth.

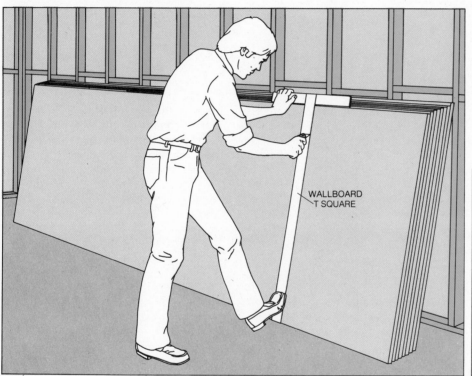

WALLBOARD T SQUARE

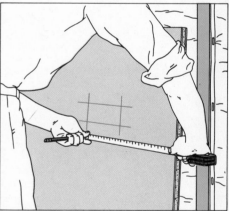

Putting Up the Ceiling

1 Applying the adhesive. Put a tube of wallboard adhesive into a caulking gun—use the large sizes for big jobs—and apply a ⅜-inch-thick bead of the adhesive to the underside of each ceiling joist that will be covered by the first board. Start and stop the adhesive 6 inches short of the point where the sides of the board will fall, so the adhesive will not ooze out at the joints between boards. Similarly apply adhesive to the edge of the joists where the ends of the board will fall, unless you plan to back-block the ends so they meet between joists (*Step 2, overleaf*).

2 **Attaching the ceiling boards.** Measure and trim the first wallboard so that its free end—the one not butted against the wall—will be directly over the midpoint of a joist or, if you are going to use back blocks, so that it will be midway between two joists. With a helper or two, lift the board into position against the adhesive-coated joists and drive a nail or screw into each joist, down the lengthwise center of the board. Then place two more rows of nails or screws through the board and into joists 8 inches in from the edge on the side adjoining the wall and ½ inch in from the edge along the free side. Fasten down the free end, if it falls on a joist, with another row of screws or nails spaced 16 inches apart. Continue in this fashion until the entire ceiling is covered.

If you are using back blocks to make it easier to conceal end-to-end joints, where the edges of the boards are not tapered, cut pieces of wallboard 8 inches wide and long enough to span the distance between joists—usually about 14 inches. Spread each piece with adhesive, using a notched trowel that produces parallel beads of adhesive about 1½ inches apart and ½ inch tall. Slip the pieces behind the free end of the wallboard panel already installed, butting them against the joist; gravity will hold them in place. Attach the next panel. Then cover the joint between the ends of the two panels with a temporary brace that will create a recess while the adhesive on the back block sets.

For the brace, press a 1-by-2 along the joint and hold it in place with three perpendicular 1-by-2s nailed to the joists on each side of the joint (*inset*). After one or two days, remove all of the 1-by-2s and fill the depression left behind by the brace with joint compound (*page 23*).

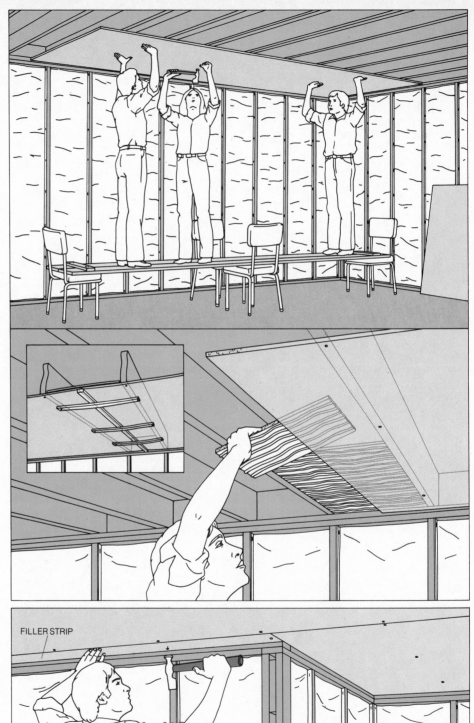

3 **Adding a filler strip.** Fill any gaps in the ceiling with strips of wallboard cut to fit and secured with adhesive and one or two fasteners driven into each joist. Omit the adhesive if the strip is less than 1 foot wide.

If the gap is adjacent to a wall, cut the filler strip from the side of a board so that it will include a tapered edge, and place the strip so that the tapered edge butts against the tapered edge of the adjoining board, assuring a smooth joint. If the gap runs parallel to the joists, cut earlier boards shorter so the filler strip will span at least two joists. Use the dull blade at the back of a dry-wall hammer like the one shown, to trim away small amounts of excess gypsum.

Putting Wall Panels in Place

1 Installing wallboard horizontally. On the ceiling and the floor, mark the positions of wall studs; these marks will serve as guides for trimming and nailing the sheets of wallboard. Apply adhesive to the studs to be covered by the first board. With a helper, lift the board into place, tight against the ceiling board at the top of the wall, then secure it, using the same fastener pattern as for ceiling boards.

To join board ends between room corners, either trim them to butt together at the midpoint of a stud or, for uninsulated walls, back-block them as with ceiling panels. If you are back-blocking, support the blocks with strips of wallboard nailed to the inner faces of studs on each side of the joint (inset). To join boards at an inside corner, butt the second board against the first and fasten the end of only the second board to a stud. At an outside corner, lap the end of the second board over the end of the first, and nail both board ends to their common stud.

When the upper course of boards is in place, install a lower one, setting boards so their joints do not align with those of the boards above. On this lower course, place fasteners ½ inch in from both edges. Add a third course if the wall is more than 8 feet tall, butting the tapered edge of the wallboard in this filler course against the tapered edge of the board above.

2 Installing vertical panels. For narrow sections of wall, install panels vertically, joining them at the midpoint of studs. Apply adhesive in the same pattern as for horizontal panels, then lift the panel into place against the ceiling, using two scraps of wood to make a foot lever. Secure the panel to each stud with fasteners spaced about 2 feet apart, starting 8 inches down from the top and ending ½ inch from the bottom.

3 **Attaching a corner bead.** To protect an outside corner, fasten a metal corner-bead strip over the wallboard joint by driving nails or screws through holes in the bead into the stud beneath. The easiest way to trim a corner bead to the correct length is to cut through the flanges with tin snips, one flange at a time.

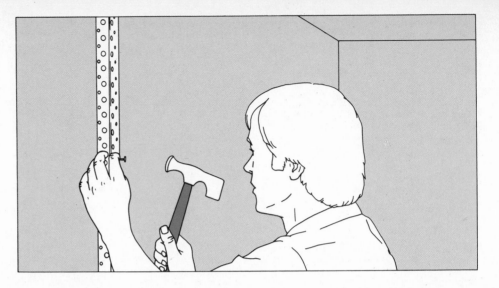

A Patch for Damaged Wallboard

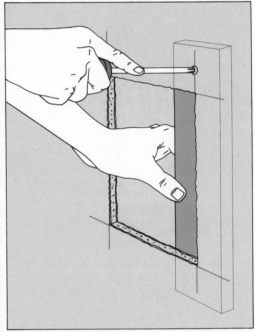

1 **Cutting out the damage.** With a carpenter's square and a pencil, draw a rectangle around the damaged area and cut along the edges of the rectangle with a wallboard or keyhole saw. To start the cut on each side, force the pointed tip of the saw blade through the wallboard, or drill holes at the corners. Pry the cut piece forward and out; do not let it drop behind the wall. Use the cut piece as a pattern for cutting a wallboard patch of the same thickness. Then cut two vertical braces for the patch from pieces of 1-by-3 lumber, making each brace about 5 inches longer than the height of the opening in the wall.

2 **Installing the braces.** Hold a 1-by-3 brace behind the wall so that it extends equally above and below the opening and is half hidden by the side of the opening. Drive a dry-wall screw through the wall and into the brace, positioning the screw in line with the side of the opening and about 1 inch above it. Drive a second screw into the brace about an inch below the opening, and additional screws, if necessary, at 8-inch intervals along the side. Install the second brace on the opposite side the same way.

Slip the wallboard patch into the opening and fasten it to the braces with screws in the four corners and every 8 inches along the sides. Cover the screws and the edges of the patch with paper tape and joint compound (*opposite*).

Finishing with Joint Compound

Seams between sheets of wallboard are concealed with a special perforated paper tape embedded in three increasingly wide swaths of wallboard joint compound. The tape reinforces the joint while the compound fills in the depression along the seam line.

For a smooth job, you will need a special pan to hold the joint compound, three wallboard knives of 5-, 8- and 12-inch widths to spread it, and a wallboard sanding plate swivel-mounted on a short pole to speed the work of sanding the compound after it is dry. For the latter, use 100-grit open-coat sandpaper.

Buy joint compound premixed, as a thick slurry. A 5-gallon container holds enough to finish the seams of about 15 4-by-12-foot boards. Professionals often vary the consistency of the three layers, adding as much as a quart of water to a 5-gallon container for the first and third layers and a pint for the second layer. You can check the consistency by dropping a glass marble into the compound from 2 feet above its surface for the first and third layers, from 3 feet for the second layer; the consistency is right when half of the marble penetrates the surface of the compound.

After use, reseal a partially used compound container. Before resealing it, however, wipe off the interior sides and smooth the surface of the compound. If the compound is not to be used again for several days, pour ½ inch of water onto its surface; pour off the water when you reopen the container.

To apply compound neatly, dip the knife sideways into the pan so you load only half the width of the blade. Keep the blade clean, especially of dried bits of compound, to avoid leaving scratches in the wet compound as you draw the knife over it. Clean the blade by drawing it over a scrap of wood, not over the edge of the pan, or debris will be continuously bothersome. Feather the outer edges of the wider second and third layers until they become paper-thin.

The first layer of joint compound is applied directly to the joint and then covered immediately with a strip of tape. At the same time, a layer of compound should cover the nailheads and the metal bead along outside corners. Before applying a subsequent layer, allow the compound to dry at least 24 hours—longer in humid weather. Sand the final layer smooth but with care, so as not to scuff the paper surface of the wallboard, since scuff marks on this surface will show through paint. If you do roughen the wallboard with sandpaper, repair the damage by applying a little joint compound with a damp sponge.

Taping to Make a Joint Stronger

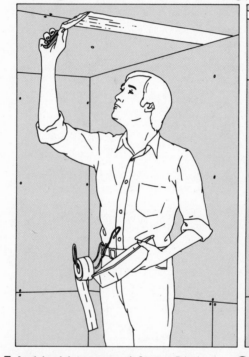

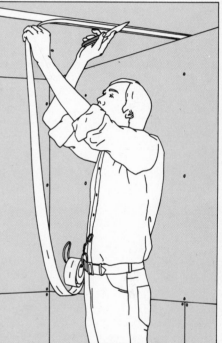

1 Applying joint compound. Scoop a 5-inch knife sideways into the compound so as to load only half the width of the blade. Center the blade over the joint, cocking the blade at a slight angle so the loaded side of the blade is the leading edge. Hold the knife almost perpendicular to the wallboard at the start of the stroke, but gradually angle it closer to the board as you draw it along the seam, forcing the compound into the depression created by the tapered edges of the board. Leave a smooth surface that more than fills the depression. Reload the knife as necessary to fill the longest seam length you can conveniently tape at one time.

For an end-to-end joint, where the boards do not have tapered edges, apply compound over the joint in a layer about ⅛ inch thick. For ease in handling the tape, bend a wire coat hanger into a V shape that will hold the roll of tape, and hook the coat hanger on your belt.

2 Embedding the tape. Center one end of the tape over one end of the joint and press it into the wet compound. Guiding the tape with one hand, run the blade of a 5-inch knife along the joint to force the tape against the compound. At the far end of the joint, press the knife into the tape and wallboard and use it as a straightedge to tear off excess tape.

Run the knife over the joint a second time, pressing firmly to push the tape into the compound and to scrape off most of the excess compound. Then go over the joint a third time, leaving a thin film of compound through which the tape can be clearly seen. See that the tape has no air bubbles beneath it and return the excess compound to the pan. At an end-to-end joint, where the paper tape rides on the surface, do not scrape out the excess compound completely. Leave a combined tape-and-compound thickness of about ⅛ inch.

3 **Applying compound to an inside corner.** Load half the width of a 5-inch knife with joint compound and run the knife along one side of the corner joint, angling the loaded edge of the knife into the corner to create a slightly thicker layer of compound right at the joint. Similarly apply compound to the other side of the joint; do not be concerned if, in applying compound to the second side, you scrape off some of the compound on the first side.

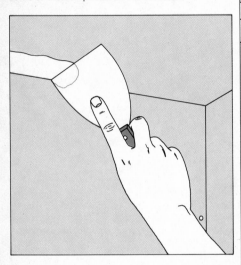

4 **Embedding tape into a corner joint.** Fold the tape along its lengthwise crease line and press it lightly into the joint compound, using your fingertips to force the crease into the corner. Begin the tape at one end of the joint and use additional lengths to reach the other end. Run the 5-inch knife blade lightly over the surface of the tape, first along one side of the crease, then along the other, just enough to make the tape stick to the compound. Then repeat, using more force to squeeze out excess compound. Finally, coat the tape lightly with some of the excess, and run the knife over it one last time, leaving a thin film of compound on the tape.

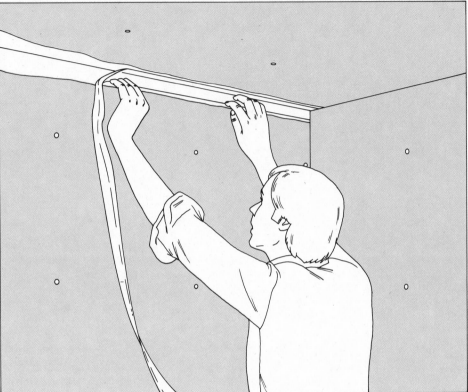

Hiding Fasteners and Joints

1 **Covering the heads of fasteners.** Load half the width of a 5-inch knife blade with joint compound and, holding the blade almost flush with the wallboard, draw the compound across a fastener head and the dimple surrounding it *(left)*. Then raise the knife blade to a more upright position and scrape off the excess with a stroke at right angles to the first *(right)*. Repeat for other fastener heads. Reload the knife with compound when there is not enough on the blade to fill the dimples completely.

Apply second and third coats in the same fashion, waiting each time until the previous coat is thoroughly dry and has shrunk the maximum amount. After the third coat the dimple should not be visible, even when the compound has dried.

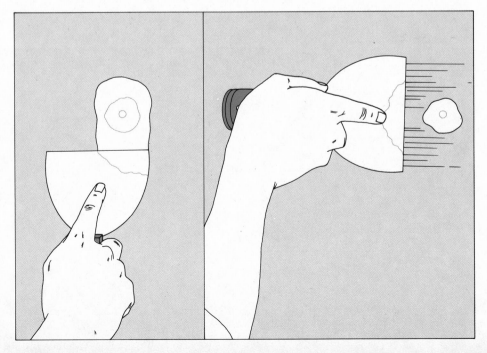

2 **Covering a corner bead.** Load about two thirds of the width of a 5-inch knife with joint compound and, lapping the knife blade about 2 inches over the corner, apply the compound by drawing the knife along one face of the bead. Repeat on the other face, then scrape off the excess compound and smooth the joint by alternately running the knife down the two faces.

Apply a second layer of joint compound, filling the knife blade two thirds full, as above, but using the full width of the knife, so as to feather the second layer out about 1½ inches beyond the edge of the first. For the third coat, use an 8-inch knife, and feather the compound out an additional 2 inches on each side.

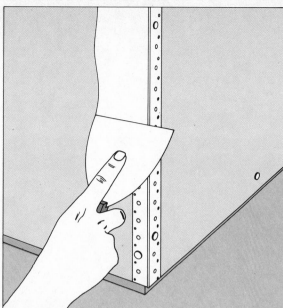

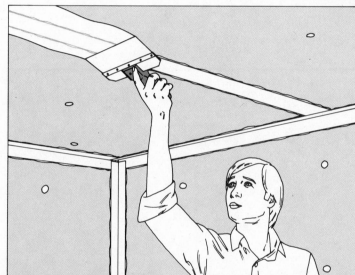

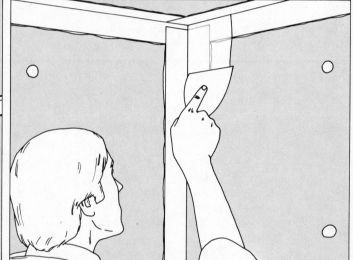

3 **Feathering a taped joint.** Load the full width of an 8-inch knife with joint compound and lay a second layer of compound over the first *(page 23, Step 1)*. Then, holding the knife slightly off center so that it laps the joint unevenly, draw the knife down the joint again. This time bear down on the knife edge that is farthest from the joint, to feather the compound on that side, and lift the other edge of the blade about ⅛ inch from the wallboard surface. Draw the knife along the joint a third time to feather the other side and create a slight ridge, roughly $1/16$ inch in height, along the actual joint line.

Apply the third layer of joint compound with a 12-inch knife. On the first pass, rest one edge of the knife blade on the ridge left by the second coat, and bear down on the other edge, thereby feathering out this last coat an additional inch or two. On the second pass, repeat this procedure on the other side of the ridge.

4 **Feathering a taped inside corner.** Load the full width of a 5-inch knife and apply the second layer of joint compound to one side of the corner. Scrape off any compound that laps onto the second side, then draw the knife down the first side again, this time bearing down on the outside edge of the knife to feather the compound. Remove any excess from the first side, leaving a smooth surface, and scrape off any compound left on the wall beyond the feathered edge. After the first side of the corner has dried, apply a second layer of compound to the second side. Then repeat this procedure with a wider, 8-inch knife for the third layer of compound.

Mastering the Art of Repairing Damaged Plaster

Although plaster is an immensely durable material—3,000-year-old plaster walls in Egyptian pyramids are still standing—it is also vulnerable to certain kinds of damage. A poorly formulated mortar mixture will result in plaster that blisters and cracks. Any plaster, if it is constantly exposed to seeping water, will eventually soften and deteriorate.

Repairing the damage is no simple matter. Plastering is an art, and a first-rate plastering job takes skill and patience. You also need to have a good working knowledge of the tools and materials of the trade and, beyond that, you need to understand enough about the various plastering techniques to choose the one best suited to your particular problem.

Every interior plaster surface consists of a base to which the plaster can adhere, and two coats of plaster. The first coat provides thickness; the second is the finishing coat, added mainly for looks. While all sorts of materials have historically been used as a base for plaster—the Romans, for example, used reeds—the base under most plaster walls today is made of metal mesh, strips of wood, or sheets of gypsum board. All of these bases are called lath.

Wood lath is generally found in houses built before 1930; in recent times, gypsum lath has largely replaced it. Similar in appearance to wallboard, gypsum lath is faced with a laminated paper chemically treated to bond with plaster. It is commonly available in sheets 16 inches wide by 48 inches long and in thicknesses of ½ or ⅜ inch. Extremely rigid and durable, gypsum lath has another advantage: Because it is as thick as some finished plaster, very little surface mortar may be needed. However, as a patching material, gypsum lath cannot be used to repair plaster that is less than $7/16$ inch thick—otherwise, the patch will protrude from the surrounding wall.

Metal lath provides the best bond for plaster, but greater skill is needed to cover it than to cover gypsum lath. While rarely used in residential construction, metal lath is ideal for repairing small holes in walls and ceilings over existing wood lath (old wood lath is usually too dry to make a good bond).

Two types of metal lath are commonly used. One is expanded-metal (diamond-mesh) lath, so called because it is made by cutting a design in a metal sheet and then stretching the sheet until a pattern of diamond-shaped holes appears. Expanded metal comes in sheets 27 inches wide, 96 inches long and ⅛ inch thick, and is best used when the plaster being patched is more than ¼ inch thick. For thinner plaster, use the other type of metal lath, woven-wire mesh, which is not only less bulky but also more flexible and therefore easier to lay flat.

With some kinds of walls the surface itself can be used as a base for the plaster; cinder block, brick and rough poured concrete, for example, do not require lath. However, such a surface must be prepared for plaster by being brushed with water, to keep it from acting like a sponge and drawing water from the plaster before it has time to set. If a concrete surface is very smooth, it must in addition be coated with a bonding agent, which provides suction for the plaster. This brush-on bonding agent is also useful for sealing edges around patches, preventing the old plaster from drawing moisture from the new before the latter has a chance to set.

Once the base has been prepared, the first layer of plaster is applied. Sometimes called the base coat, it is made by adding water to a premixed combination of perlite and gypsum plaster, which is spread over the lath or masonry to a depth slightly less than the thickness of the surrounding plaster. A trowel is used to create a level but rough-textured surface.

The second coat, called the finish coat, determines the appearance of the wall or ceiling and thus must be smoother and of a finer texture. It is made of a mortar that spreads more easily, consisting of 3 parts Type S hydrated lime mixed with 1 part finely ground gauging plaster and 1 part water; the lime adds plasticity to the mixture. Most finish coats are simply trow-eled smooth, but sometimes you will have to add cosmetic touches to make the patch match the surrounding plaster, texturing the surface randomly or uniformly with any of a variety of tools, ranging from sponges to special trowels.

Whatever the finish on the original plaster—smooth, rough or textured—if it is damaged, you will need to assess the extent of the damage before beginning the patch. Scratch through the surface to the base coat with a sharp tool. If it takes considerable pressure to make a mark on the base coat, the underlying plaster is still good enough to be left as it is, and only the finish coat will need to be patched. Simply scrape off the loose surface plaster with a trowel, brush a bonding agent on the good plaster beneath, and apply two coats of finishing plaster. For the first coat, add a small amount of fine sand—about 5 to 10 per cent of the total bulk—to the gauging plaster, to roughen it slightly.

If the base coat is also in bad condition, it is probable that the lath beneath it will also have to be patched, if only to provide a dependable base for the new plaster. Wood lath dries out with age and gypsum lath loses its ability to provide a good bond. In most cases, it is simplest to leave the old lath in place and put new lath over it. Only if the old lath is badly broken or distintegrated will you need to remove it entirely and install new lath directly on the wall studs or ceiling joists.

For all patching jobs, certain precautions should be observed. Make sure the environmental conditions are right: Temperature can greatly affect the setting of plaster. The room temperature should be between 55° and 70° for 24 hours prior to the plastering and until the plaster has set. There should be adequate ventilation, but no direct breezes. Finally, because finish plaster contains lime, which can burn your skin and eyes, wear gloves and a long-sleeved shirt and cover your eyes with goggles—especially if you are working on a ceiling. It is also advisable to wear a respirator when you are tearing down old plaster.

Tools of the Plastering Trade

Assembling the right equipment. To do a professional job of making a large patch in a plaster surface, you will need some general-purpose tools and several specialized ones. Most can usually be found at stores that handle building supplies or at hardware stores.

Essential for any plastering job is a hawk, typically a 12-inch-by-12-inch sheet of metal with a detachable wooden handle centered and fixed to its underside; it is used to hold the mortar, that is, the moist plaster. You will also need a rectangular trowel, made of tempered high-carbon or stainless steel, for applying, spreading, shaping and smoothing the mortar. Either a pointed trowel or a margin trowel (a smaller version of the rectangular trowel) is useful for spreading mortar where the larger trowel will not fit and for cleaning other tools. In addition, for mixing the mortar, you will need a plastic mortar box or a wheelbarrow and hoe, and a 4-by-4 piece of plywood to serve as a mortarboard.

Though professional plasterers use a wide variety of tools to level and smooth mortar, three are usually sufficient for patching jobs. One is a strip of aluminum called a slicker, or rod; here, it is not drawn in scale with the other tools, since it is 4 feet long, 6 inches wide and ⅛ inch thick. The second is a metal angle float, a trowel-like tool with flanged edges, used for smoothing plaster along an inside corner. Good for roughening the base coat in preparation for a finish coat is a steel-tined comb, called a scarifier.

When patching ornamental plaster, a small pointing tool made of stainless steel is useful for filling cracks or chips. And to duplicate the surrounding textured surfaces on patches of new plaster, you may need one or more of the following: a stippling (or dash) brush, a sponge float, or simply a rectangular sponge.

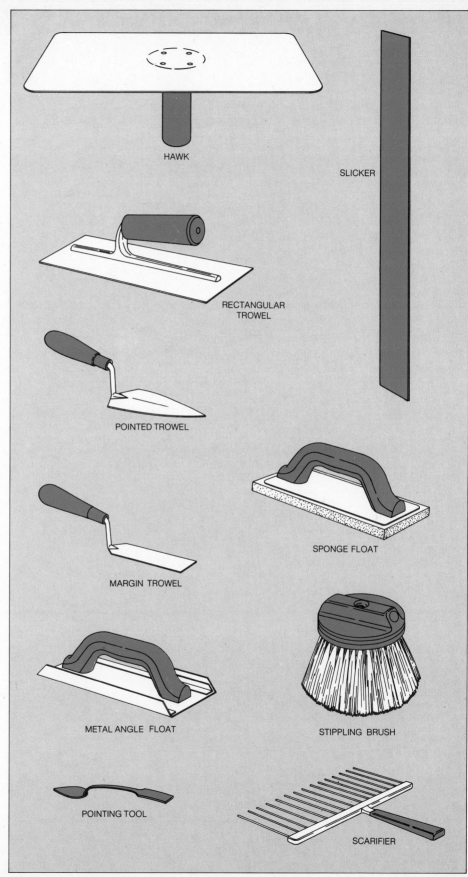

HAWK

SLICKER

RECTANGULAR TROWEL

POINTED TROWEL

SPONGE FLOAT

MARGIN TROWEL

METAL ANGLE FLOAT

STIPPLING BRUSH

POINTING TOOL

SCARIFIER

Providing a Solid Base of Gypsum or Metal Lath

Installing gypsum lath. To repair large holes spanning studs or joists, first pry off any loose plaster with a putty knife and, using a magnetic stud finder if necessary, find the two studs or joists nearest the edge of the damaged area. Draw a rectangle around the area, using the centers of the studs or joists as sides of the rectangle, connected top and bottom at right angles. Score the rectangle with a utility knife and chip away the plaster down to the lath with a hammer and cold chisel. Mark the position of any framing members uncovered in the process—studs, joists, firestops and spacers—on the good plaster at the edges of the opening.

Cut gypsum lath to fit the opening, using the same techniques as for wallboard (*page 19*). With the specially treated side (the side that is covered completely with paper) of the gypsum lath facing toward you, nail it in place with $5/16$-inch-head lath nails long enough to penetrate the wood support at least ¾ inch. Place the nails ½ inch from the edges of the board and 5 or 6 inches apart. If you install more than one piece of lath, leave a small gap, no more than ¼ inch wide between boards and stagger the end joints. Cover these joints with metal-lath stripping.

Before applying any mortar, brush the edges of the old plaster and about 5 inches of the surface adjoining those edges with a thick coat of bonding agent. Wait about an hour, until the bonding agent becomes tacky, before plastering.

Installing metal lath. To make a smaller patch over existing wood lath, first pry off any loose plaster with a putty knife, and with hammer and cold chisel create an opening that extends slightly into sound plaster; the opening can be any shape. With tin snips, cut a piece of metal lath to fit the opening and nail this lath to the underlying wood lath with fourpenny box nails, placed at 3-inch intervals.

If you are patching a corner, where two walls are damaged, cut a piece of lath to fit one surface and lap onto the other about 2 inches. On the edge of a worktable, bend the lath to fit around the corner. Cut a second piece of lath to fit the adjoining wall and overlap the first piece 1 inch. Set the two patches in place (*inset*), fastening their lapped ends together with 18-gauge tie wire.

Brush the edges and about 5 inches of the face of the sound old plaster with a thick coat of bonding agent. Wait for it to dry until tacky before you begin applying plaster.

Strengthening the weak spots. Wherever plaster has a tendency to crack or be damaged by impact, reinforce the gypsum lath with special strips of 26-gauge galvanized-steel or zinc-alloy mesh. These come in three styles, for different situations, and in lengths ranging up to 12 feet. They can be trimmed to size with tin snips. Fasten the strips to the lath with 1⅛-inch nails, placing the nails in the center and at 12-inch intervals.

On an outside corner, use the angled metal-mesh strip that has a rounded bead along its edge (*below, left*). This "corner bead," nailed plumb over the corner, not only acts as a bumper but serves as a guide in applying the plaster, ensuring a straight corner line.

On an inside corner, use a strip of "cornerite"— angled metal mesh with no bead (*below, center*).

On a flat surface where movement of structural supports within the wall may cause the plaster to crack, use flat reinforcing mesh, called stripite (*below, right*). Place the stripite diagonally across the damaged part of the wall, where it will have the effect of bracing the plaster over the structural members that are prone to movement—as, for instance, the framing that is adjacent to the top corners of a door.

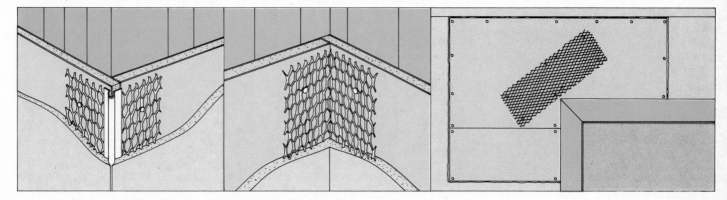

Preparing Mortar and Applying the Base Coat

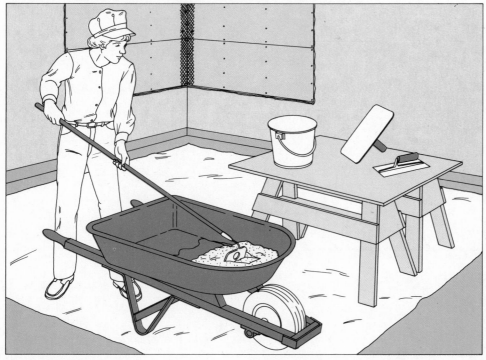

1 Mixing the base mortar. For patches requiring large amounts of mortar, use a wheelbarrow and hoe to mix the dry material with water. Pour the dry material into a pile at one end of the barrow, and put water in the other end. Gradually pull the dry material into the water with the hoe, using short, choppy strokes at first, then lengthening the strokes as you work farther into the pile. With each stroke, cut through to the bottom of the barrow. Add more water as needed, until the mixture has the consistency of

soft butter. Transfer the mixture, a bucketful at a time, to a mortarboard—a 4-foot-by-4-foot piece of plywood—and use the forward end (the toe) of a rectangular trowel to chop through the mixture to break up any remaining lumps.

For patches that will require smaller amounts of mortar, mix the dry material with water in a plastic mortar box. Transfer this mixture, too, to a mortarboard for the final smoothing of the mixture with the toe of a trowel.

2 Cutting a hawkful of mortar. Use a rectangular trowel to transfer mortar from the mortarboard to the hawk. First separate from the pile a section of mortar about half the size of the hawk and push it toward the hawk, at the same time pushing the hawk toward the trowel. As the edges of the hawk and the trowel meet, sandwich the mortar between them, tilt them both slightly upward and scoop the mortar up onto the center of the hawk. Trim off any excess mortar with the trowel.

3 **Troweling the mortar.** Tip the hawk toward you and use the long edge of the trowel to cut a slice of mortar from the far edge of the pile *(below, left)*. Place the trowel against the bottom edge of the patch, with the trowel's long edge touching the wall and its face angled slightly outward. Then, in one smooth motion, sweep the trowel upward *(below, right)*, forcing the mortar against the wall until the trowel is empty. As you cut out each slice of mortar, give the hawk a quarter turn, so the pile remains centered.

Apply the mortar in a layer no more than ½ inch thick. If additional mortar is needed to bring the base coat to within 1/16 inch of the wall surface, allow the first layer to set for several minutes before applying a second.

When you are troweling mortar onto a ceiling, do not stand directly beneath the trowel. Falling mortar might land in your face.

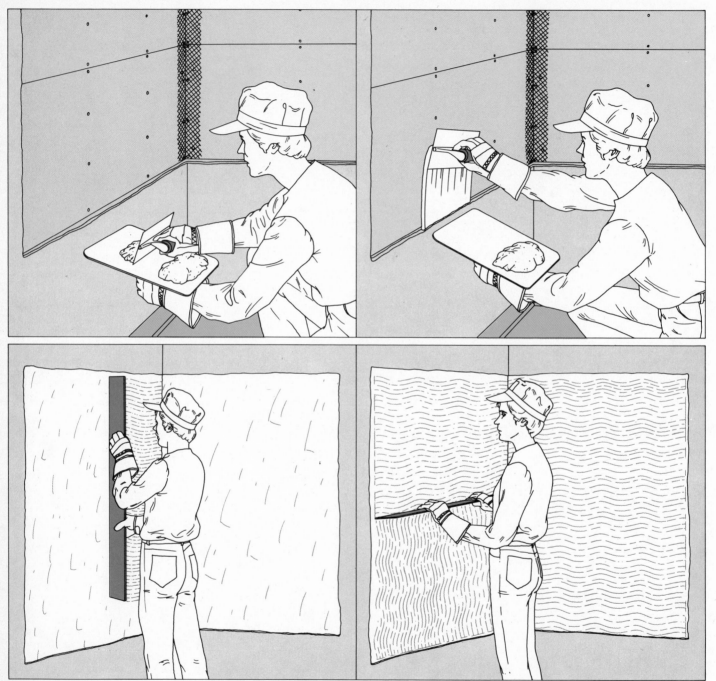

4 **Making the surface even.** Wet the slicker and, holding it vertical with the long edge against the wet mortar, draw it across the patch *(above, left)*. Begin at the corner if there is one; if not, start at either side. As you move across the mortar, shift the slicker slightly up and down, leaving a wavy pattern in the mortar. This up-and-down motion keeps mortar from building up on the edge of the slicker.

Repeat this smoothing action in parallel, slightly overlapping rows until you reach the bottom edge of the patch. Then hold the slicker horizontally *(above, right)* and go over the patch from bottom to top in the same way, leaving behind a pattern of wavy lines running at right angles to the first. Hold the slicker at a slight slant to let excess water and soft plaster flow off one end.

30

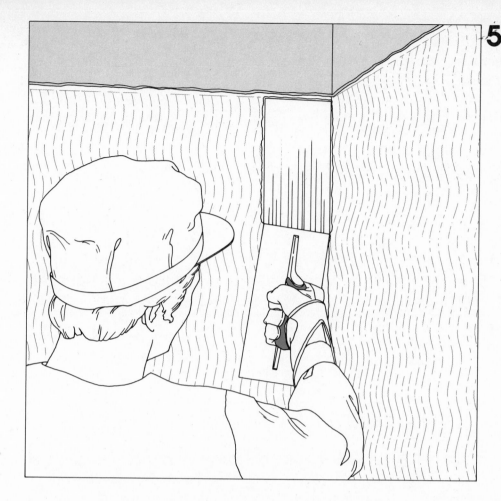

5 **Trimming the rough spots.** To remove excess mortar from an inside corner, draw the toe of the trowel first down one surface, then down the other. On an outside corner, use the rounded nose of the corner bead as a guide; it should be free of mortar. Make sure the mortar level of the patch is 1/16 inch below the surface of the old plaster, to allow for the depth of the finish coat.

Let the base coat set for several minutes, then roughen the entire surface with a scarifier or the tip of a pointed trowel. Wait 24 hours, until the base coat has set—when a trowel dragged over it will make a squeaking sound, like that of chalk on a blackboard. Then scrape down any remaining high spots with a trowel.

Applying the Finish Coat

1 **Mixing the finish mortar.** On a 4-foot-by-4-foot mortarboard supported by sawhorses, mix the mortar in the following proportions: 3 parts lime, 1 part gauging plaster and 1 part water. First put 1 gallon of water in a 5-gallon bucket and mix in hydrated lime until the mixture has the consistency of soft butter. Place this mixture on the mortarboard and chop it with the toe of a clean, wet rectangular trowel to break up lumps; then shape the lime into a ring.

Pour clean water into the ring and, with a flour sifter or square of screening, sift gauging plaster into the water until all the water is absorbed. Do not stir while you sift; stirring hastens the setting. Let the mixture rest for a minute, then cut out a wedge of the plaster and lime, and use the trowel to mix them into mortar.

Because finishing plaster sets so quickly, have a helper mix the mortar while you apply it. Also have a bucket of water handy for cleaning tools, and line up all your tools in advance on the mortarboard. You will need a rectangular trowel, a margin trowel or pointing trowel, and a hawk.

2 Troweling the finish coat. Starting at the top of the patch and working down, spread a thin layer of plaster over the scarified base coat, using the same technique as in troweling the base coat. Cover only a small section (about 2 feet by 2 feet) at a time and, without waiting for the first layer of the finish coat to set, apply a second layer, bringing the section up to the level of the surrounding surface.

As each section is completed, square any inside corner with a metal angle float, running the float down the two surfaces (*inset*). Tilt the float so its toe barely touches the plaster and its heel rides slightly above the plaster. Fill in any blemishes—"cat faces"—with a pointed trowel.

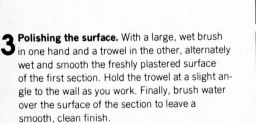

3 Polishing the surface. With a large, wet brush in one hand and a trowel in the other, alternately wet and smooth the freshly plastered surface of the first section. Hold the trowel at a slight angle to the wall as you work. Finally, brush water over the surface of the section to leave a smooth, clean finish.

Repeat Steps 2 and 3 for each section. As each new section is added, use the wet brush to blend the edges of sections together.

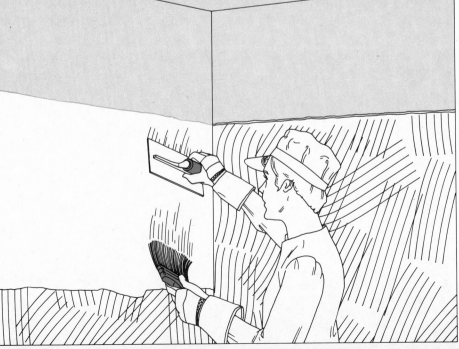

Special Treatments to Texture the Surface

A sand finish. In mixing the mortar for a sandy finish coat, blend 2 parts 16-mesh silica sand with 1 part gauging plaster, and combine with water as for a base mortar (*Step 1, page 29*). Apply in the same way as for a smooth finish but as each section is completed, dash a small amount of water on the plaster and rub it in a circular motion with a sponge float to bring the sand grains into sharp relief.

Stippled and swirled finishes. Apply a thin first layer of finish mortar as in Step 2 opposite, and roughen it with a scarifier. Then dip a stippling or dash brush into the mortar on the hawk and daub it over the first layer. Space the daubs so the texture of the patch matches that of the surrounding wall. To achieve a swirl finish (*top inset*), give the stippling brush a sharp twist as it touches the surface of the plaster. For a rougher, more random texture (*bottom inset*), use long, overlapping strokes.

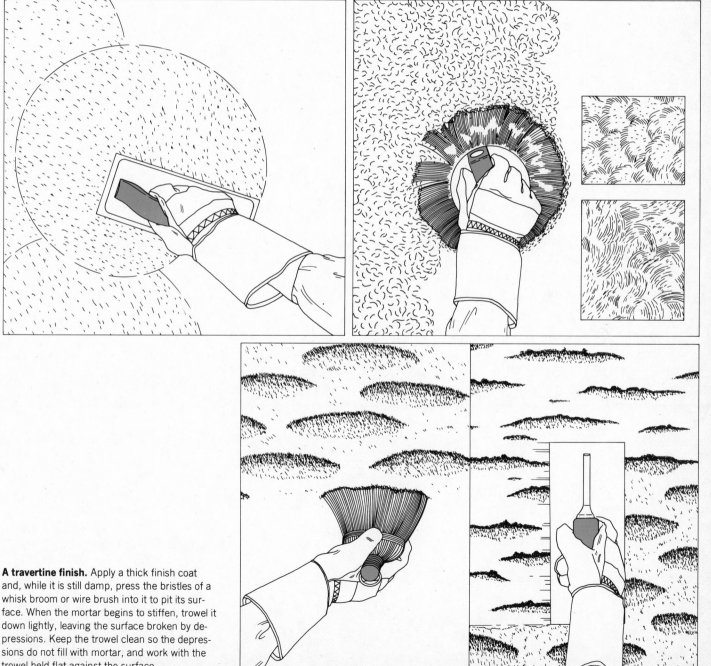

A travertine finish. Apply a thick finish coat and, while it is still damp, press the bristles of a whisk broom or wire brush into it to pit its surface. When the mortar begins to stiffen, trowel it down lightly, leaving the surface broken by depressions. Keep the trowel clean so the depressions do not fill with mortar, and work with the trowel held flat against the surface.

Adding Moldings and Medallions

Artisans have been affixing plaster decorations to walls for centuries, mostly in imitation of Greek and Roman bas-relief. In modern times, the practice peaked in the early 19th Century, when Greek Revival architecture reawakened an interest in classical ornamentation.

Today, plaster moldings are again popular, either to give authenticity to a restoration or just to add interest to an otherwise flat wall. The designs offered, most of them from old pattern books, range from chaste Greek-key borders to Baroque ceiling medallions. Many lumberyards and hardware stores carry smaller pieces, but most of the larger, more elaborate patterns must be ordered from craft studios or manufacturers.

Moldings and medallions are also available in pressed wood or plastic (a lightweight urethane), and are installed like plaster, but plaster is more authentic and usually has better detail. Moreover, plaster can be patched if it chips or cracks, and rough areas are easily sanded smooth. Ordinary panel adhesive is used to hold the plaster pieces in place; nails or wood screws support the pieces until the adhesive dries.

The most commonly used plaster ornament is a ceiling medallion used as a foil for a chandelier. It comes with a wiring hole that is covered by the chandelier's ceiling plate. Since these plates vary in size, choose a medallion with a hole of the proper diameter. (Medallions are also made without center holes, for decorating a ceiling without a chandelier.)

Before removing the chandelier to make way for the medallion, turn off the power to the chandelier at the circuit-breaker or fuse panel; simply turning the wall switch to OFF may not give you complete protection. Then disconnect the chandelier from its electrical box in the ceiling and temporarily seal off the wire ends with wire caps. After the medallion is installed, reverse this process to reinstall the chandelier.

Most ceiling medallions are predrilled to accommodate a pair of mounting screws. For those that are not, drill two ⅛-inch holes, opposite one another, near the medallion rim; then countersink the holes so the screwheads will be hidden. Use No. 12 screws in plaster or wallboard, but if the plaster of a ceiling is crumbly, substitute Molly anchors.

Along with ceiling medallions, another popular plaster trim is the molding used to frame the wall space above a fireplace, sometimes called a chimney piece. Before beginning such an installation, check the wall for evenness; plaster strips are not pliable. Shims can sometimes be used to level two strips meeting on a bowed wall, but only if the difference between them is less than ¼ inch. Also, because the strip patterns must match precisely at the mitered corners, select a simple design to make matching easier.

To lay out the position of these framing strips, use a rule, carpenter's level and chalk line to establish a rectangle whose sides are plumb and whose top and bottom are parallel. Transfer the chalk-line measurements onto the plaster strips to mark the distance between miter cuts. Careful positioning of these marks will assure a cut that passes through the middle of the pattern, for a neat miter joint.

In addition to common tools, you will need a small amount of patching plaster, a plasterer's pointing tool (page 27), and painter's caulk. The patching plaster should be mixed to the consistency of oatmeal and shaped to the surrounding design with the two ends of the pointing tool, used alternately.

Possibilities for plaster ornaments. Plaster moldings can be used to decorate a room in a variety of ways. Here, a ceiling medallion highlights a chandelier; cornice molding softens the juncture of walls and ceiling; border strips frame an area above the fireplace; and the fireplace itself is set off by a plaster mantel. Other available plaster ornaments include plaster door trim and decorative ceiling panels that imitate everything from coffers to festoons and shields.

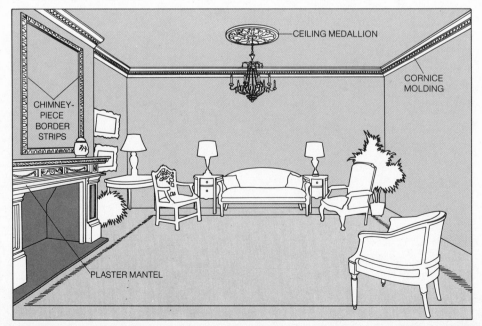

A Chandelier Decoration

1 **Marking the medallion position.** For a medallion used with a chandelier, turn off the power at the circuit breaker, remove the chandelier and center the hole in the medallion over the electrical box, using the hole in the crossbar of the box as a reference point. Scribe a line around the medallion and mark for the screw holes. If the medallion design contains squares or rectangles, be sure they are parallel with the walls and mark their position on the circle lightly in pencil.

In a room without a ceiling fixture, position a solid medallion by locating the center of the ceiling. Snap a string—powdered with colored chalk dust only near its middle—between the two sets of diagonally opposite corners. Tie a pencil to one end of a string the length of the radius of the medallion. Pin the other end of the string to the ceiling at the intersecting chalk marks. Then use this pencil compass to draw a circle on the ceiling corresponding to the medallion rim.

With a caulking gun, ring the back of the medallion with 2-inch-wide daubs of panel adhesive, spacing them 2 inches apart.

SCREW HOLE

2 **Attaching the medallion.** Press the medallion against the ceiling, aligning it carefully with the guidelines you marked in pencil. Then, with a helper holding the medallion, fasten it to the ceiling with wood screws. Use a pointing tool to fill in the screw holes with patching plaster; smooth the plaster patches with a wet paintbrush. Fill a caulking gun with a tube of painter's caulk and apply caulking around the outer rim of the medallion. Use a wet paintbrush to smooth this joint too. When the plaster has dried, paint the medallion with white ceiling paint or another color of your choice. Finally, rehang the chandelier and turn the power back on.

Creating a Border for a Chimney Piece

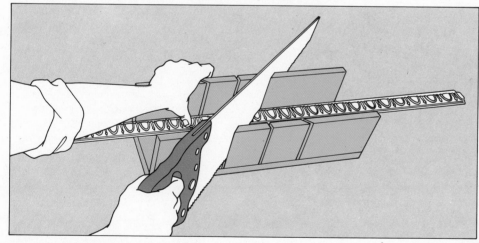

1 **Mitering plaster molding.** Lay a border strip face up in a miter box and cut the strip at a 45° angle. Use a wood saw with widely spaced teeth so that the saw will not become clogged with plaster. In selecting the place to make the cut, keep in mind that the design has to match neatly at the corners; you may need to alter the dimensions of your chimney border slightly so that the corner cuts will fall at the right points in the molding design.

After all four strips are cut, lay them on the floor to check the match at the corners. Then apply daubs of panel adhesive to the backs of the strips, spacing the daubs about 1 foot apart.

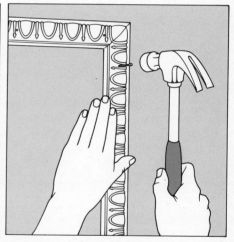

2 **Positioning strips on the wall.** Place the strips along the chalk lines that mark the inner edge of the chimney piece. Nail them in place, using sixpenny galvanized finishing nails, countersinking their heads. Fill the holes and any gaps at the corners with patching plaster, using the pointing tool to shape the plaster to the surrounding design. Use painter's caulk in a caulking gun to fill the inside and outside edges of the strips. When the plaster is dry, paint the trim.

If the wall is bowed so that two mitered strips do not meet on the same level, shim the lower strip to raise it a bit from the wall. Caulk the gap and smooth with a wet paintbrush.

2

Fresh Old Walls, Easy New Walls

A facing of tiles. Swirls of mastic raked across wallboard provide an adhesive for squares of ceramic tiles. The measured notches on the trowel distribute the adhesive evenly and a pyramidal sequence in setting the tiles helps to keep each row straight and true. When every square is in place, the designs on these imported tiles form bold and colorful patterns.

Because of their visual prominence—and perhaps because they surround us so much of the time—walls invite decoration. In past centuries, indoor walls held much the same allure for the artist as a freshly stretched square of blank canvas. Working on still-moist lime plaster, the great fresco painters of the Renaissance executed both commonplace murals and extraordinary masterpieces on the interior walls of churches, public buildings and palatial residences. At an even earlier time, artisans working in the homes of wealthy patrons carved bas-reliefs on walls or inlaid wall surfaces with intricate, colorful patterns of mosaic tile.

In our own era, styles of wall decoration have become simpler. For a time modern architects took a starkly functional approach to the design of houses, emphasizing clean, uncluttered lines and rejecting most forms of wall ornamentation as dust-catching gingerbread. Largely as a result of this attitude, bare wallboard walls are still accepted almost without question in many new homes today.

But a moderate swing in the opposite direction is under way. Architects and decorators are once again indulging in wall coverings that add pattern, color and texture. While the designs of new houses remain simple and functional, these wall coverings add a new visual interest—an extra step that earlier generations took very much for granted. New materials have been developed and old ones revived to meet this demand for decoration.

Ceramic tile is an ancient material, but it is now produced in an enormous variety of shapes, colors, sizes and designs. Special adhesives make the installation of ceramic tile a project for the amateur as well as the skilled craftsman.

Mirrors, like tiles, are hardly a modern innovation. But recent improvements in the technology of glassmaking have made it possible to produce large panels of quality mirror at affordable prices. Whole walls can now be faced with mirrors, dramatically transforming not only the wall but the entire room. Equally dramatic are the patterns and textures of cork—a wall covering that not only enhances the appearance of a room but also makes it quiet. Even a brick wall can be realistically simulated with lightweight facings of clay-fired or plastic brick.

You can go a step beyond resurfacing a wall and add a new wall altogether. Building materials such as metal studs that connect like a child's construction set and tie into existing house framing make it easy for the home craftsman to add new interior partitions. By creating fresh faces for old walls or new shapes for some of your existing rooms, you can dramatically change not only the style of your home but your style of living as well.

A Durable, Handsome Armor of Ceramic Tile

Ceramic tile has been admired for centuries as a sheathing for walls. Durable, water-resistant and easy to clean, tiles have adorned Persian mosques, Moorish palaces and the parlors of Dutch burghers. Today, although they are mainly associated with kitchens and bathrooms, where their practicality outshines their other virtues, ceramic tiles are by no means strictly utilitarian. They come in an inspiring array of colors, shapes and sizes.

When you shop for tiles, it is well to remember that they also come in several basic forms. They are available glazed and unglazed, for instance. Unglazed tiles, dull rather than glossy, are usually laid on floors—although nothing precludes their use on walls. Tiles also are available in different weights—lighter for walls, heavier for floors. And though tiles are commonly sold individually, some can be purchased in sheet form; the tiles are joined together either by a flexible grout or by flexible plastic or paper mesh. Sheet tiles can save you considerable installation time, especially if the individual tiles are small.

Whether purchased in sheets or individually, tiles are generally sold by the square foot. The one exception is trim, the specially shaped pieces that are used to go around corners and to finish edges. These are sold by the running foot. Make sure that you have both measurements—square feet and linear feet—in hand when you estimate your tile needs. Add a little extra to your estimate to allow for breakage during installation and for making future repairs.

Before installing tiles, you must provide suitably flat backing surfaces. Then, working directly on the walls, you must plan the arrangement of the tiles to minimize slight variations from true in the backing surfaces, and to avoid as much as possible the need for odd-sized tiles. Finally, in setting the tiles, you must choose an adhesive that is compatible with the backing material.

Traditionally, tilesetters believed that the only suitable backing for tiles was a thick bed of mortar, called mud in the trade. With the development of thin-set adhesives, however, all sorts of surfaces provide suitable backings for tiles—gypsum wallboard, plaster, plywood, mason-ry, concrete, laminated plastic, even old ceramic tile itself. The only requirement is that the backing surface be stable and flat, with no more than ⅛ inch of distortion over a span of 8 feet.

In many cases the only preparation the surface will need is a thorough cleaning and some minor repairs. Cracks should be filled, loose paint or wallpaper removed, and glass-smooth surfaces roughened with sandpaper. If you plan to tile over existing tile, make sure all the old tiles are securely anchored. If some are loosened—by water damage to the backing, for example—you will have to tear down the backing and replace it.

Whenever an existing backing is unsuitable—due to water damage, bad cracks or a bumpy or irregular surface—use the techniques illustrated on pages 11-32 to replace it. Commonly the replacement will be wallboard. If you need to install a new backing around tubs or stall showers, be sure the wallboard is water-resistant or, better yet, use composition board especially developed for areas exposed to moisture. Technically known as concrete, glass-fiber-reinforced backer board, this product is marketed under the trade name Wonder-Board, and is installed in much the same way as ordinary wallboard (pages 18-25).

Once the backing surface for the tiles is prepared, you can begin to lay out their placement, establishing guidelines for level rows and the starting point for setting the first tile. The placement of this tile is critical since it dictates the position of all other tiles on the wall.

Some professionals begin tiling a wall by setting a full tile in the most visually prominent corner; thereafter they vary the space between tiles to control the sizes of cut tiles at the opposite corner. A more predictable method, shown opposite, assures you of tiles of equal size at both ends of the row and lets you avoid having to cut very narrow end pieces.

The rows themselves are generally leveled by measuring up from the base of the wall and establishing a level guideline (opposite, top right). However, if the tiles surround a tub, the first row of full tiles should in many cases be set less than one tile width above the rim of the tub. Sometimes a tub will settle at one corner, causing the rim to slope. In such a case you will have to cut border tiles one by one to fit between full tiles and the tub (page 41, Steps 1 and 2).

In the choice of adhesives, there are a number of options. Thin-set adhesives are designed for almost any type of backing, but you must read the labels with care because the adhesives have varying characteristics. Cement-based adhesives, which are mixed with water, work well on wallboard, for instance, but not on wood, which tends to swell due to the water content. Organic adhesives, called mastics, need no mixing and work well on most common backing materials.

Not all mastics are alike, however. Those called Type I mastics are designed to resist water; until they harden, they are flammable and may harm skin and lungs, so use them with caution and in a well-ventilated room. Type II mastics, compounded with latex, are easier to handle but less durable in wet areas. Both types come in formulations for walls and for floors, with different setting times—wall mastics harden less rapidly, allowing more time for positioning tiles.

After the adhesive has set, tile joints must be filled with grout to protect the backing from water. Grouts can be decorative—they come in many colors—and they too have different formulations. The most common grouts are cement-based, but silicone grout can be used with some tiles. Ask your tile dealer which grout is best for your particular installation.

For setting tiles you will need a carpenter's level, a steel ruler, a chalk line for establishing guidelines, and a notched trowel for applying the adhesive. The notches should have the correct spacing and depth for the tile and adhesive selected, as prescribed by the manufacturers. For applying cement-based grouts to vertical surfaces, the best tool is a rubber-faced float. Silicone grouts, however, are applied with a caulking gun.

For the job of cutting tiles, you may be able to rent a ceramic-tile cutter with a scoring wheel like that of a glass cutter. For odd shapes and holes, you will need tile nippers. Finally, to protect yourself, wear goggles when you cut tile, and rubber gloves when you work with grout or with Type I mastic adhesive.

Establishing a Level Starting Line

Making a layout stick. Line up a row of tiles—evenly spaced as they will appear on the wall—along a straight piece of 1-by-2 lumber, 3 to 4 feet long. Mark the width of each tile along this board, allowing a space for a grout joint at either end. If the tiles have built-in spacer lugs along their edges, butt the lugs together to achieve the proper gap. But if the tiles have no spacer lugs, experiment to find the most pleasing spacing for the grout lines—usually between $1/16$ and $1/8$ inch—and maintain this spacing across the layout stick.

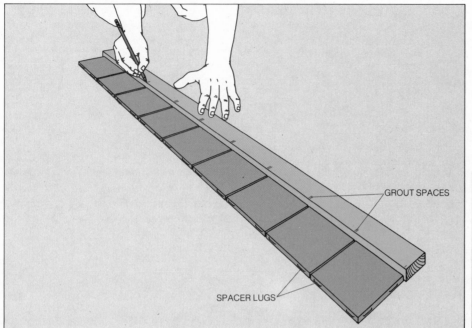

GROUT SPACES

SPACER LUGS

Establishing guidelines. Using a carpenter's level, draw a guideline near the base of the wall for the first row of tiles. To determine the position of this line, locate the lowest point along the floor with the aid of the carpenter's level, then prop a base-trim tile and a full wall tile against the wall at this point, separating them by a grouting space. Rest the carpenter's level on top of the second tile (outside the spacer lugs, if any) and use the bottom edge of the level to establish the guideline. Continue the line across the wall with a straightedge or by snapping a chalk line, checking it for accuracy with the level.

Measure to locate the midpoint of the line and place the layout stick against it, lining up the midpoint with a tile-edge mark. Slide the stick along the line until you reach the corner. If your last space is less than a half tile wide, adjust the tile positions by moving the midpoint a half-tile width off center. Use the level to draw a vertical guideline through the selected midpoint.

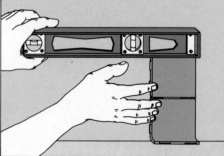

Plotting the Guidelines for Tiling around a Tub

1 **Determining the starting point.** Measure up from each corner of the tub with the layout stick and mark the desired height of the tiled wall; remember that the tiling should extend at least a full tile above the shower head. Draw a level line from each mark toward the adjacent corners; the lines will meet if the tub edge is level.

If the tub is within $1/8$ inch of being level, use the technique shown above to establish a guideline for the first row of tiles, using the high point of the tub as a reference point, and fill the space between the bottom tiles and the edge of the tub with grout. If the tub is more than $1/8$ inch out of level, establish the guideline from the lowest point along the tub and fill the uneven space at the tub edge with a row of tiles trimmed to fit.

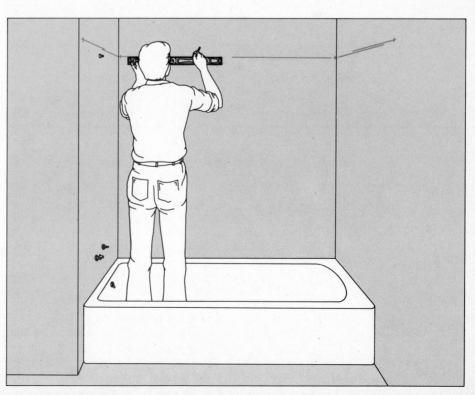

2 Adjusting the guidelines. If you plan to carry the tiles on the end wall of a tub all the way to a front corner, you will need to find out if that corner is plumb. Hold a tile against the guideline where it intersects the front corner; the tile and the corner should line up. If they do not, adjust the guideline as follows, to compensate for the deviation *(right, top)*: Tilt the tile to align with the corner, then hold a chalk line beneath the tile's lower edge with one end tacked on the original guideline at the far corner, raising or lowering the tile as necessary but keeping it aligned with the corner. Snap a line of chalk and use it as the new guideline.

To turn a guideline around a corner onto an adjacent wall *(right, below)*, hold the layout stick against the corner, lining up one of the tile marks with the existing guideline at the end of the tub. Mark the top of the first full tile near the base of the adjacent wall. Then, with the aid of a carpenter's level, extend the mark into a horizontal guideline across the wall.

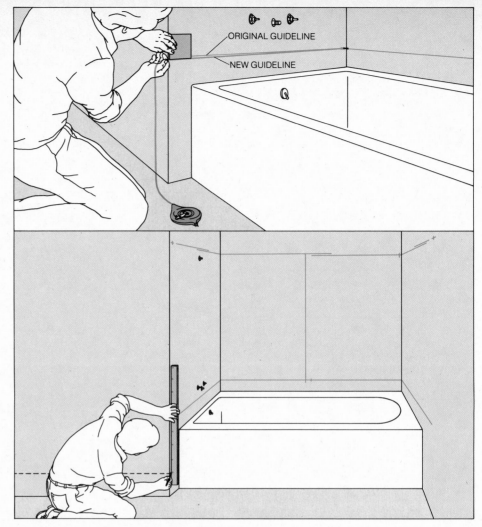

ORIGINAL GUIDELINE

NEW GUIDELINE

Setting the Tiles in Place

1 Applying the adhesive. Using the straight edge of a notched trowel, spread adhesive in a thin, even coat over a 12-square-foot area next to the intersection of vertical and horizontal guidelines; be careful not to cover the lines. Then turn the trowel and, holding the notched edge at a 45° angle to the wall, rake over the adhesive, applying firm pressure against the backing.

When you have gained practice at setting the tiles, you can expand the working area to cover more than 12 square feet at a time.

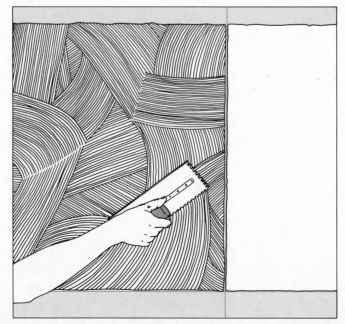

2 Placing the tiles. Set the first tile in the corner formed by the intersecting guidelines, and subsequent tiles in the numbered sequence shown on the tile faces in the drawing, to form a pyramid. As you set each tile, twist it slightly to sink it firmly in the adhesive, but avoid sliding it into place as this clogs the space between tiles, which must later be filled with grout.

If the tiles tend to slip out of place before the mastic hardens, ensure proper spacing by tapping sixpenny finishing nails beneath them. Tiles with spacer lugs will need nails beneath tiles only in the bottom row, but tiles without lugs may need support nails beneath every tile.

If you are setting handmade tiles that are slightly irregular in shape or size, center each one as accurately as possible over the horizontal and vertical center lines of adjacent tiles. If a tile is slightly bowed—a common flaw in handmade tiles—use the short edge of the trowel to put some adhesive on the tile as well as the wall, so that no part of any tile lacks adhesive.

To set a running-bond pattern (*inset*), center the first tile over the vertical guideline. Again, follow the numbered sequence to build the tiles out in horizontal rows, but stagger each row by centering each tile over the joint between the two tiles already in place directly beneath it.

3 Leveling the tiles. While the adhesive is still tacky, remove any support nails and, using a hammer and a cloth-padded scrap of wood or the rubber-faced float used in grouting, tap on the face of each tile until it sits deep in the adhesive and lines up with the plane of surrounding tiles. Within an hour, clear the grout joints of any adhesive that has been forced into them, and clean adhesive from the faces of the tiles, using water or the solvent recommended by the adhesive manufacturer.

Cutting Tiles to Fit Narrow Spaces

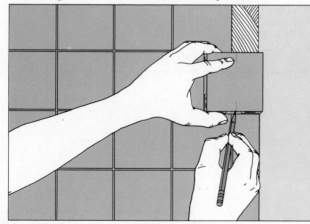

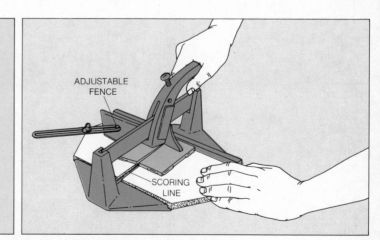

1 Marking the tile. Hold the tile to be cut, finished side up, so that it butts against the tub or adjoining wall and overlaps the last full tile in its row. Mark the border tile along both edges, so that the cut will reflect any irregularities in the space to be filled; allow space for grout. If the tiles have ridges on their backs, position the tile so that the cut runs parallel to the ridges.

2 Trimming the tile. Wearing goggles, slide the tile into a rented tile cutter and align the marks on the edges of the tile with the scoring line on the base of the tool. Snug the adjustable fence against the edge of the tile. Push the handle forward to run the scoring wheel across the tile, then tip the handle back and force it down sharply to snap the tile along the scored line.

Cutting Tiles to Fit around Pipes

1 Marking the position. If a pipe protruding from the wall must pass through the middle of a tile, hold the tile in position directly below the pipe and mark the location of the center of the pipe on the edge of the tile. Then cut the tile in two. Hold each cut section in position on opposite sides of the pipe and mark the width of the pipe on each cut edge.

If the pipe is at the edge or corner of a tile, use the same method to mark its position. To make an edge or corner hole, however, there is no need to cut the tile in two.

2 Nipping out the hole. Wearing goggles and holding the marked tile with the glazed side up, use tile nipppers to nibble tile away within the marks, gradually roughing out a hole for the pipe. Test for fit as you go but do not try to smooth the cut edge since the escutcheons usually hide ragged cuts. Where they do not, and a more precisely cut hole is required, mark the dimensions of the pipe on the back of a tile. Place the tile, with its glazed side down, on a scrap of wood and steady it by surrounding it with nails driven partway into the wood. Then cut the hole along the marked line, using an electric drill with a carbide-tipped hole-saw accessory (*inset*).

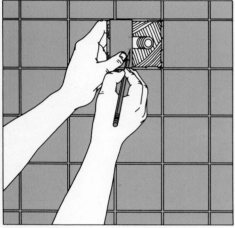

Grouting to Finish the Job

1 Applying grout. Wearing rubber gloves, mix cement-based grout to the consistency specified by the manufacturer and trowel it onto the tile surface with a rubber-faced float. Force the grout into the tile joints with crisscrossing diagonal strokes of the float edge, up and down across the tiles. When all of the tile joints are filled with grout—including those at the corners and top and bottom edges—sweep over the tiles with the edge of the float to remove as much grout as possible from the tile surfaces.

2 Smoothing the joints. Allow cement-based grout to dry for 10 minutes. Then soak a sponge in clear water, wring it well and wipe the tile surface with a circular motion. Rinse the sponge frequently in a bucket of water; do not rinse in the tub or lavatory as the grout might clog the drains. Continue rubbing the tiles until most of the excess has been removed and the grout in the joints is very smooth. Let the wall dry until its surface is hazy. Then polish the tiles with a soft, dry cloth and tool away any rough points in the grout with the handle of an old toothbrush.

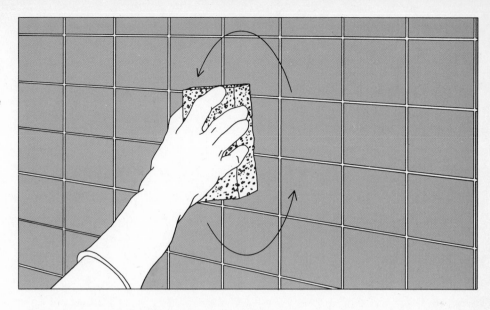

Pregrouted Tile Sheets for Faster Installation

Fitting the sheets. Tack straight-edged scraps of wood just beneath the horizontal guideline to give temporary support to the bottom tier of sheets. Then apply adhesive and set sheets on the wall, maintaining even spacing between the sheets by butting together the spacer lugs. To fit a sheet around a pipe, cut out the whole tile over the pipe and trim away the flexible grout that held the tile in place on the sheet. Then cut the individual tile to fit around the pipe as shown in Steps 1 and 2, opposite, top. For border areas, remove and trim individual tiles in the same fashion, then mark and cut them to size as shown on page 41, Steps 1 and 2.

Using a caulking gun and a tube of silicone grout with the tip cut at a 45° angle, fill the joints between sheets to the same depth as the pregrouted tiles. Clean smudged grout from the surface of the tiles with alcohol and a soft cloth.

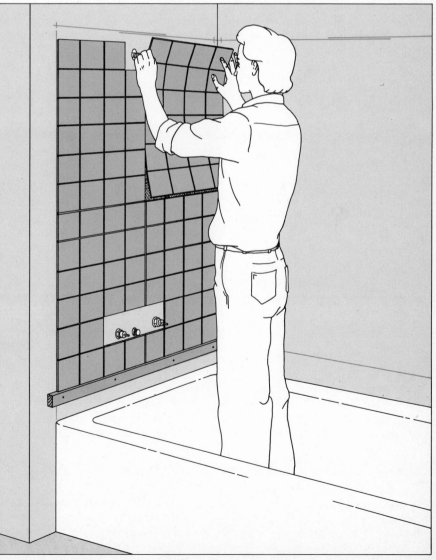

Mirrored Walls to Brighten a Room

If you cannot put your favorite easy chair beside a window that commands a view of the garden—or a glimpse of the city skyline—a strategically placed wall of mirrors may reroute the prized view into the interior of your home. Mirrored walls also increase the apparent size of cramped rooms and bolster limited sunlight. But the mirrors must be securely installed to avoid damage and carefully aligned so the image is not distorted.

Mirrors in every form—framed, backed with hardboard or unbacked—have traditionally been attached to the wall with hardware clips, tracks or hangers. Properly executed, such installations are safe and reliable. They provide space behind mirrors for ventilation that prevents moisture from discoloring the silvering. Perhaps most important, they make mirrors easy to remove should you decide to leave one house for another or redecorate a room. Some useful examples of traditional mirror hardware are shown on pages 46 and 47.

In some modern installations, however, the edges of mirror panels are butted together, leaving no room for standard hardware. One fastening solution for such designs is the use of rosette clips (page 46), which screw into holes drilled through the mirrors or into notches cut into the mirror corners. More commonly, mirror panels are installed with an adhesive. Such an installation is called structural by the professionals—it makes the mirrors a permanent part of the wall. But it also makes them difficult to remove intact, so consider well before installing mirrors in this way.

The simplest of structural installations makes use of lightweight, 1-foot-square mirror tiles, widely available at hardware and department stores. These thin glass tiles have the advantage of being the only type of mirror that you can cut yourself. All other mirrors are thicker and require professional cutting.

The recommended adhesive for lightweight mirror tiles is a double-faced tape that is sold both in rolls and in precut squares. Apply this tape only to smooth, very clean surfaces and do not attempt to use it on vinyl wall coverings. Once you peel off the protective cover, hold the tape only by its edges—even the oils of your skin can cause this tape to fail.

The thin glass that makes mirror tiles light in weight also tends to lessen their reflective quality. For a more distortion-free reflection, you will need a thicker, more expensive mirror, and to install such a mirror you will have to use a mastic adhesive, one compounded specifically for the job of hanging mirrors.

These special mastics are made of materials that do not react with the silver on the mirror, and are applied in such a way that they never dry out entirely. Because it retains some resiliency, the mastic can withstand sudden jolts—even a minor earthquake—that might otherwise jar the mirror loose. Application techniques are designed to foster this resiliency by keeping each pat of mastic distinct and intact while covering 60 per cent of the wall surface. A wooden application tool is used because it is less likely to scratch the mirror backing.

When you buy a mastic, ask the mirror dealer to recommend the one most suitable for your job. Most mastics can be used only with hardware clips. Some require unusual preparation of the backing surface, such as coverage with a special bonding coat. Read label directions carefully.

Work with mirrored panels calls for some precautions. Because good-quality mirror stock is heavy, a large unbacked panel is awkward and fragile; leave the installation of panels larger than 12 square feet (2-by-6 or 3-by-4 feet) to professionals. When you carry a large mirror, work with a helper and carry the panel vertically; if held horizontally it might crack of its own weight. If a mirror does slip from your grasp, do not attempt to catch it. Just get out of the way.

Although mirrors may be mounted wall-to-wall and floor-to-ceiling, you will find that your installation is simplified if you plan to leave at least a narrow border of uncovered wall. Tailoring mirrors to fit irregularities can be difficult. With all that is reflected in the mirror itself, the presence of an unmirrored border usually goes unnoticed.

Mirror Tiles: Low-Cost and Easy-to-Install

1 Laying out mirror tiles. Using the straight edge of a carpenter's level, draw crossed guidelines for positioning level rows of 12-inch mirror squares. To establish the vertical guideline, measure the width of the wall surface to be tiled. If this width is an even number of 1-foot segments or measures slightly more or less than an even number of feet, make a mark at the midpoint of the wall. If the width of the area to be tiled is an odd number of 1-foot segments, make the mark at a full-foot measure to either side of the midpoint. Draw a vertical line through this mark to the upper and lower edges of the area to be tiled, making it plumb with the level or using a chalk line and plumb bob.

Measuring down from the top of the vertical line, make a mark at the 1-foot measure closest to your eye level. Draw a level line horizontally through this mark to the ends of the tile area.

Unpack the mirror tiles and prepare an adhesive tab by peeling off one side of its protective cover. Press the tab firmly to the backing of a tile ¾ inch in from a corner; repeat at the other corners, then on the other tiles.

3 Cutting border tiles. Measure the width of the border and transfer this measurement onto the face of a tile, using a felt-tip pen to mark the cutting line. With the mirror face up, on a workbench, lay a straightedge along this cutting line and use a glass cutter to score the line in one smooth motion. For best results, wedge the cutter between your first and second fingers, start the scoring wheel $1/16$ inch in from one edge of the tile and apply even pressure as you draw the wheel across the glass. Do not go back over the scored line.

Wearing heavy gloves and goggles, grasp the tile by its opposite edges, scored side facing away from you, and gently snap the tile in two. Fix squares of tape in the corners of the cut tile and press it firmly on the wall.

2 Setting the tiles. Strip the outer paper from the tabs on the first tile, line up its edges against one corner of the guidelines, then press the mirror against the wall, applying firm pressure to its corners. Set subsequent tiles in rows, working outward from the center of the wall.

Before attaching each tile, test it for fit with its adhesive tabs still covered. If a tile does not fit exactly flush against the edges of both adjoining tiles, remove the tile temporarily and place a strip of ½-inch-wide black plastic tape on the wall, butted against one of the two adjoining tiles. Then set the imperfect tile permanently in place, lining up one edge but leaving a slight gap along the edge that is camouflaged by the tape. Install all of the full mirror tiles, leaving until last any area that might require cut tiles.

Beveled Mirror Panels Held with Mastic

1 **A dry run on the floor.** On a carpet or drop-cloth, lay out all of the panels as they will be placed on the wall. Pad every joint between two mirrors by lining one of the square edges (not the visible bevel) with a strip of masking tape. Use ½-inch tape and fold the excess onto the back of the mirror *(inset, top)*. This will cushion the edges so glass will not rub on glass, should any movement occur. If you plan to fasten the panels to the wall with both mastic and rosette clips, use grozing pliers or tile nippers to chip ⅛ inch from each corner where four panels meet.

With all of the panels laid in position, measure the edge that will be at the bottom of the installation. Use a hacksaw to cut a section of metal J molding *(inset, bottom)* to this length, tapering the ends of the molding slightly inward from bottom to top. With a carpenter's level, draw a guideline for the molding and fasten it to the wall, at the studs, with sixpenny nails. Cover the nailheads with masking tape to keep them from scratching the mirror backing, and pad the bottom of the channel with bits of rubber or felt.

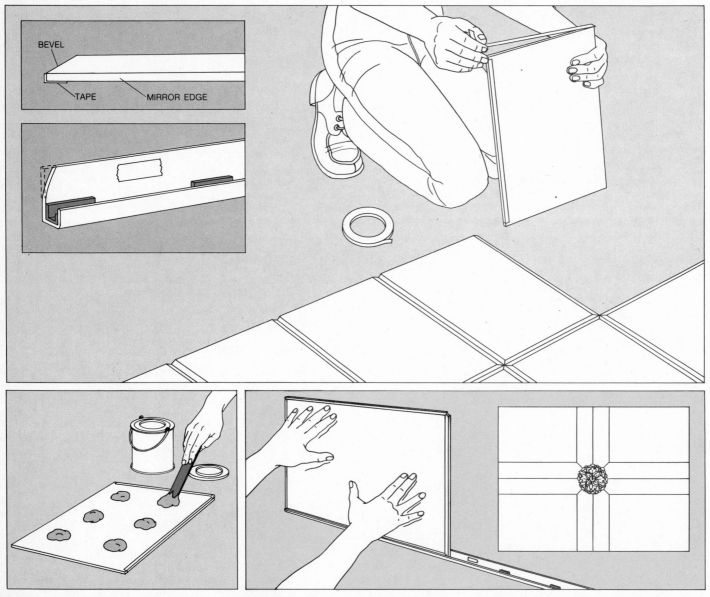

2 **Applying mirror mastic.** Use a wooden paint paddle or any small scrap of wood with a smooth end to daub pats of mastic onto the back of the mirror. For every square foot of mirror, apply four pats of mastic roughly 1½ inches square and ⅞ inch thick. Keep the mastic at least 2½ inches from the edges of the mirror. If mastic begins to harden on the daubing stick, discard the stick and use a clean one.

3 **Installing the panels.** Set the bottom edge of the first mirror panel into the channel at one end of the J molding, then press the mirror back against the wall. Apply uniform pressure to the surface of the mirror until the mastic flattens and the tile is approximately ¼ inch away from the wall. Repeat this procedure to install a second panel flush against the edge of the first and at a uniform depth in the mastic. Complete the bottom row of panels before you begin installing those in the rows above.

If you are using rosette clips *(inset)*, drill a ³⁄₁₆-inch hole for a 1-inch-long plastic anchor, centering the hole where the corners of the tiles would have met if you had not clipped them. Insert the plastic anchor flush with the surface of the wall. Install the rosettes with 1¼-inch screws.

Larger Mirrors Held with Mastic and Clips

1 Supports for big mirrors. Draw a level guide-line along the bottom of the wall you will be panel-ing and mark the positions of the mirror panels along this line. Using screws and plastic anchors, install two clear-plastic J clips for the bottom of each mirror, spacing them equidistant from the panel-edge marks and equidistant from each other. If you use steel J clips instead of plastic clips, pad the clips *(page 46, Step 1)*. Cover all screwheads with masking tape.

Measure up from the bottom guideline to mark a line for the tops of the mirrors, checking with a carpenter's level. Above each clip on the bottom line, install an adjustable top clip *(inset)*, set-ting the clips level with the line in their closed po-sition. Attach them to the wall with screws, then raise the adjustable top channels, opening them fully to allow insertion of the mirror.

For every square foot of mirror, apply four pats of mastic in $\frac{7}{8}$-inch thicknesses, $2\frac{1}{2}$ inches away from the edge of the mirrors.

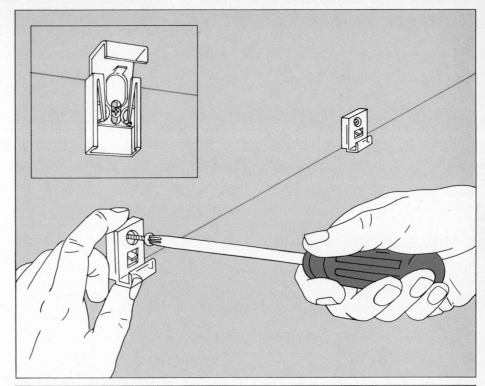

2 Mounting the mirror panels. With a helper holding one edge of the mastic-daubed mirror and supporting its face, tilt the top of the mirror forward slightly and lift the bottom into the J clips. Tilt the mirror back against the wall. Starting at the bottom, apply even pressure over the entire mirror surface, forcing it against the mastic until the panel is a uniform $\frac{1}{4}$ inch away from the wall, and the top edge of the panel is resting against its clips. Slide the adjustable top clips down over the edge of the mirror.

Place each subsequent mirror panel with its edge against the edge of the last one installed. Press the panels evenly into the mastic so their reflecting surfaces form a perfectly flat plane.

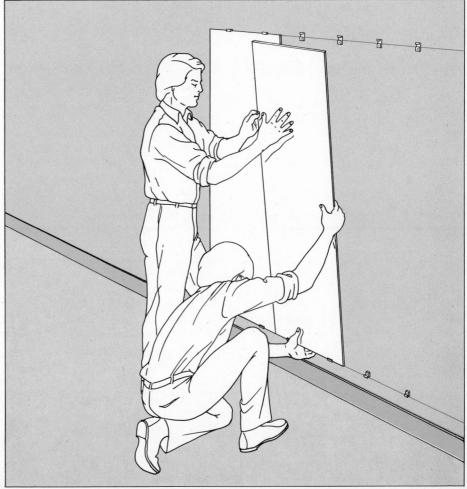

Using Cork as a Wall Covering

Cork, the bark of an oak species that grows chiefly along the Mediterranean in Spain and Portugal, is among the most handsome and versatile of all wall coverings. It comes in textures ranging from the familiar fine-grained cork used for bulletin boards to exotic designs of woven, fissured or marbleized cork—available mostly through shops that cater to professional decorators.

Cork walls complement fine furnishings. In a practical vein, they can serve as message centers in kitchens or other workrooms and as buffers around the dart board in a game room. They are easy to install and maintain, and provide excellent insulation against heat and sound.

The many cork textures available are the results of different processing methods. Some of the natural bark is simply sliced into sheets or slabs, rather like plywood. More often it is ground up into chunks or granules and then reconstituted and formed into rolls, sheets or slabs. Cork wall covering sold in sheet form is flexible and usually no more than ¼ inch thick. Hardware stores generally sell it in bulletin board-sized rolls, typically 2 feet by 3 feet, or 4 feet by 6 feet; 3- or 4-foot-wide bulk rolls, which can be cut to size, are available at some lumberyards. In slab form, wall cork is commonly cut into square or rectangular tiles and is sold at hardware or wall-covering stores.

Cork tiles come in many colors in addition to shades of brown, in many patterns, and with squared or beveled edges. Their thickness usually varies from ⅛ to ¾ inch, their size from 1 foot square to 1 foot by 3 feet. Although most tiles are made of solid cork—sometimes several layers glued together—others have a wood or fiberboard backing.

The tiles are sold either plain or with a pressure-sensitive adhesive backing that makes them easy to install: You simply peel off their paper and stick them in place on the wall. But you pay a premium for this convenience, so self-adhering tiles are economical only in small areas.

Because cork is porous, it expands and contracts with changes in humidity. To prevent a change of size after your cork is on the wall, unpack it and leave it for at least 72 hours in the room in which it is to be installed. If it is in sheet form, unroll the sheets and weight them down to flatten them as much as possible. And when they are glued into place, butt the sheets or tiles together without forcing them, and leave a bit of leeway for the cork to expand in damp weather.

Most manufacturers recommend that cork be applied to the wall with a water-soluble, latex-based adhesive of the type used in laying linoleum floor tile. However, if the cork is being installed where it might be subjected to moisture, as on the interior of an exterior masonry wall, use an alcohol-based adhesive, which is impervious to moisture once it has set. To form a uniform bond, the adhesive should be spread evenly and completely over the wall with a notched trowel, preferably one with V-shaped notches ¹⁄₁₆ to ⅛ inch apart.

The surface to which cork is applied must be dry, flat and dust-free. Cinder block and similar porous materials should be coated with a sealer to prevent moisture from reaching the cork, and shiny surfaces such as high-gloss enamel paint should be roughened with sandpaper. If you want your cork wall to be temporary, you can mount it on a portable surface— on a plywood panel, for instance, or a wall divider *(pages 58-61)*. Once in place, cork is almost impossible to remove without damaging not only the cork but also the wall surface.

Cork tiles are usually arranged in a checkerboard pattern, like ceramic tiles, and a layout for their placement should be plotted in the same way *(pages 39-41)*. Except for wood-backed tiles, which must be cut with a fine-toothed saw, most cork can be cut with a utility knife or a single-edged razor blade. You can, if you like, give the completed cork wall a protective coating of sealer, stain, varnish, wax or polish, so you will be able to use liquid cleaners on it. In its unsealed state, cork is cleaned with the brush attachment of a vacuum cleaner.

Surfacing a Wall with Square Cork Tiles

1 Cutting cork. Using a steel square or straight-edge as a guide, cut cork with a utility knife or a single-edged razor blade. To prevent breakage, first stick masking tape on the cork. To fit cork around irregular objects, make a paper pattern, then trace a cutting line onto the cork with chalk. When you cut, protect the work surface with hardboard or heavy cardboard.

To ensure smoothly fitting tiles, check the edges of all tiles with a square, trimming them if necessary. If a tile breaks during installation, glue the pieces together on the wall; because of the cork's texture, the break will not show.

2 Pressing the tiles flat. After you have set all the tiles in place against the adhesive, run a rolling pin over them. Apply firm, even pressure to remove all air bubbles and to force the back of each tile tight against the wall. Pay special attention to the edges of the tiles, where a poor bond would be most noticeable. Run the rolling pin over the tiles diagonally.

To keep especially thick or rough-textured tiles flat against the wall, drive finishing nails partway into all four corners of each tile and into the center. After the adhesive sets, either remove the nails, using a scrap of wood under the head of the hammer to keep from damaging the cork surface, or use a nail set to drive the nails into the crevices of the cork.

Mounting Large Sheets of Cork

Tacking up temporary strips. As you lay sheet cork against the adhesive-covered wall, nail strips of scrap wood or plywood near any curling edges of the cork to hold it flat until the adhesive sets. On long stretches of cork, place such strips every 6 feet or so—or as close together as necessary to keep the cork from pulling away from the wall.

After the adhesive has set, remove the strips. To finish cork that does not cover the entire wall, frame it with thin L-shaped corner moldings.

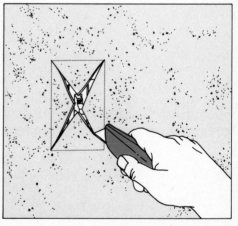

Trimming around a switch or outlet. When you cover a wall with thin, flexible cork, remove the faceplates of outlets and switches and apply the cork directly over the openings. After the cork sheet is glued in place, find the openings by feel and, with the power turned off, cut a small X in the center of each. Carefully enlarge the X, using the corners of the electrical box as a guide, then trim the cork to match the edges. When the adhesive is completely dry, replace the faceplates, using slightly longer screws if necessary to allow for the thickness of the cork.

The Realistic Beauty of a Thin Brick Veneer

In the vast array of wall surfaces available to homeowners, one of the most intriguing is brick veneer. These thin slabs of kiln-fired clay—cut in ½-inch slices from full-sized bricks or molded individually to the same thinness—add the warmth, color and rough-hewn charm of brick to almost any room, at a fraction of the cost and weight of solid masonry. In fact, they are competitively priced with the many imitation-brick facings made of plastic or plaster-based compounds *(page 55)*.

Veneer bricks are installed in courses like full-sized bricks, and the spaces between them are filled with real mortar for a look of authenticity. They come in two forms: either as individual bricks or as preassembled brick panels that normally contain 36 bricks arranged in six courses of six bricks each and measure 16½ by 48 inches. The panels, fastened to the wall with nails, are speedier to install.

But panel brick veneer has disadvantages. It is heavy, requiring two people to set each 30-pound panel into place. It can be mounted on any structurally sound surface, but if the surface is dry wall, the framing studs behind that surface must not be more than 16 inches apart, center to center. Panel brick veneer is also more expensive than individual veneer bricks, and the backing material, asphalt-impregnated fiberboard, is not fireproof. The panels are difficult to fit around obstacles such as doors and windows; they are most useful on large uninterrupted walls. Finally, the panels are available only in a running-bond pattern.

Individual veneer bricks, on the other hand, come in many colors and finishes and can be arranged in whatever pattern you choose. They come both flat and shaped. The shaped bricks, used on corners and edges, usually include an L-shaped unit that combines the side and end of a brick; a V-shaped unit that combines the top and side; and a three-sided unit that combines side, top and end.

The flat bricks are the size and shape of the side of a brick used lengthwise, commonly called a stretcher; they are usually about 7½ inches long and 2¼ inches high. To form a header—to give the appearance of a brick turned sideways and seen end-on—you simply cut a stretcher brick in half with tile nippers.

Veneer bricks are attached to the wall with a synthetic-rubber cement, and will adhere to almost any smooth surface. The wall should be clean and free of wallpaper; if painted, it should be scored with a pointed tool to roughen the surface for the adhesive. Other preliminaries include removing the baseboards, although window and door trim can be left in place. The faceplates of electric outlets and wall switches should also be removed and their outlet boxes extended with special collars *(page 17)*, so that the faceplates, when replaced, will lie flush on the new surface.

While installing the bricks, have a bucket of water handy for rinsing your tools and for washing excess adhesive from the face of the bricks. The excess adhesive can also be removed when dry, with mineral spirits.

Although the bricks themselves are fireproof, check with local authorities before installing them near a stove or fireplace. Some fire codes require that they be backed with a fireproof material such as metal, asbestos or cement-base panels. (If you use an asbestos product, wear a protective mask.)

Like real bricks, veneer bricks can be cleaned with a masonry cleaner such as trisodium phosphate. In areas where grease deposits are a problem, protect the bricks with a clear masonry sealer.

Mimicking the Look of Real Brick

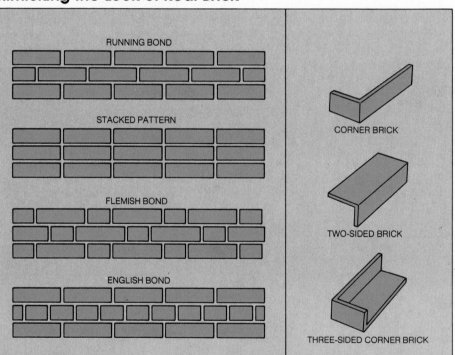

RUNNING BOND

STACKED PATTERN

FLEMISH BOND

ENGLISH BOND

CORNER BRICK

TWO-SIDED BRICK

THREE-SIDED CORNER BRICK

Choosing a pattern. Veneer bricks can be laid in almost any pattern used for structural brick walls. Most common is the traditional running-bond pattern, in which stretcher bricks are set in staggered rows, or courses. Other popular designs are the stacked pattern, in which stretcher bricks are set in vertical columns for a contemporary look, and two patterns in which stretcher bricks are combined with half-sized header bricks. (These last two patterns, Flemish bond and English bond, are derived from Colonial houses in which header bricks joined the two layers of a double brick wall.) Specially shaped bricks *(above, right)* are used at corners and edges.

The number of bricks needed for each pattern varies, but is generally six or seven bricks per square foot. To estimate your needs exactly, lay out your pattern on the floor next to the wall for which it is intended, leaving ⅜ to ½ inch between the bricks for mortar. This dry run before the installation will allow you to adjust the spacing between bricks, minimizing the number of bricks that must be cut to fit.

Setting Individual Bricks

1 Measuring and marking courses. For an installation that covers an entire wall without interruption, mark the position of horizontal courses along one end of the wall, beginning at the floor line. If the floor is not level, start at the higher end. If a window or door interrupts the wall, use the top of the window frame or doorframe, or the bottom of the window frame, as a starting point, so that one full brick and its mortar joint will abut the edge of the frame. To allow room for a ½-inch mortar joint between courses, space the courses 2¾ inches apart.

Tap a nail into one of the marks and wrap a chalked string around it. Have a helper hold the string taut against the far end of the wall while you check the position of the string with a line level. When the string is level, snap it; the line this leaves on the wall will mark the top of the first course. Measure and snap off additional chalk lines, using the first line as a guide.

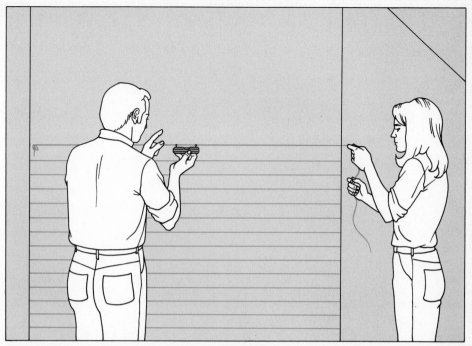

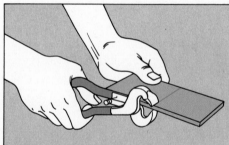

2 Cutting bricks to fit the pattern. To create header bricks or to cut bricks into smaller sizes to fill gaps where the pattern abuts an obstacle, draw a pencil line across the back of the brick where the cut will be and grip the edge of the brick with tile nippers. Align the blades with the pencil line and cut. Smooth the cut by chipping away any rough edges with the nippers. Always wear safety goggles when cutting bricks.

3 Establishing the pattern. Starting at an inside or outside corner of the wall, set a line of bricks up the wall from bottom to top, lining up the top of each brick with the chalk guidelines. On an inside corner, use header and stretcher bricks, alternating them as the pattern requires; wrap outside corners with L-shaped bricks (inset).

With a putty knife, apply adhesive to the back of each brick in ¾-inch daubs, about ½ inch thick and 2 inches apart. Press the brick against the wall with a slight twisting motion to spread the adhesive, which will ooze out around the edges of the brick. Tap 1½-inch finishing nails partway into the wall beneath L-shaped bricks to hold them in place until the adhesive sets, in about 48 to 72 hours; then remove the nails.

Applying Brick Veneer to Irregular Areas

Outlining an arch. Using L-shaped bricks with either the stretcher side or the header side facing out, set the bricks against the curve of the arch. Begin by setting one brick in the exact center of the arch and one on each end. Working on one half of the arch at a time, fill in the area between the center brick and the ends, spacing the bricks to keep the V-shaped mortar joints uniform in width. Apply adhesive as in Step 3, page 51. Use 1½-inch finishing nails tapped partway in at an angle to hold the bricks in place until the adhesive sets.

Framing a raised hearth apron. Cap the corners of the hearth with three-sided corner bricks, then set bricks combining stretcher and top surfaces along the edges of the hearth. Space the bricks evenly across the front edge, adjusting the distance between them as necessary to avoid cutting any bricks. Set bricks along the side edges in the same way.

With the framing bricks in place, set L-shaped bricks on the front edges of the apron. Fill in the apron in the pattern of your choice.

Filling Joints with Mortar

1 **Applying the mortar.** After the adhesive has set, remove the supporting nails and fill in the spaces between the bricks with thin mortar applied with a mortar bag—a cone-shaped container of heavy canvas fitted with a ½-inch nozzle through which you squeeze the mortar by rolling down the top of the cone. Squeeze enough mortar into the joints so the mortar bulges out slightly beyond the face of the brick; like decorating a cake with a pastry bag, this takes some practice. Fill the horizontal joints first, then go back and fill the vertical. Rinse out the mortar bag between refillings.

Use a ready-mix mortar enriched with 1 or 2 tablespoons of liquid detergent to keep the mixture flowing smoothly from the bag. Or you can mix the mortar from scratch, using 2½ parts sand to 1 part portland cement. Add enough water to thin the mixture to the consistency of applesauce; this is thinner than for conventional bricklaying, where the mortar has to support the weight of a brick. To eliminate lumps, sift the dry mix through a scrap of window screen before you begin mixing it with water.

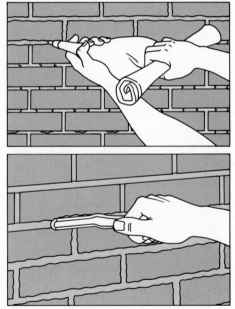

2 **Tooling the joints.** After about 20 minutes, when the mortar is dry and crumbly to the touch, smooth and flatten it so that its surface lies about ⅛ inch below the face of the brick. For this job, use a ½-inch jointer, a mason's tool with a convex surface that presses the mortar in against the edges of the bricks. Tool the vertical joints first, then the horizontal ones. Use the jointer to scrape off any excess mortar while it is still soft. When the mortar is completely dry, usually within 1 or 2 hours, rub the bricks and joints vigorously with a stiff-bristle or wire brush to clean them of mortar remnants.

Nailing Up Panels of Brick Veneer

1 Providing a base for corner bricks. Nail framing strips of ½-inch-thick fiberboard or plywood to the corner of the wall, up to the desired height of the brick paneling. Set one strip flush with the corner and lap the other strip over it. To produce two framing surfaces of equal width, make the second strip ½ inch wider than the first. The width of the framing strips may vary with each manufacturer's panel assembly; follow the instructions that are printed on the package.

2 Nailing the panels to the wall. Starting at the base of the wall, butt the backing board of one panel against the corner framing strip and nail the panel to the wall along the edge nearest the corner. On plaster or wallboard walls, use 1½-inch roofing nails and drive the nails into wall studs; on concrete-block walls, use fluted-shank masonry nails. Place the nails between the bricks and, using a nail set, drive them flush with the surface of the backing board. To make sure this and subsequent panels are level, snap a level chalk line across the wall 16½ inches above the floor and use it as a guide.

3 **Interlocking the panels.** Have a helper pull the unattached edge of the first panel away from the wall just enough to let you slide the adjoining panel into it until the two backing boards meet; then push both panels against the wall. Nail the second panel to the wall along the joining edge, as in Step 2, and complete the nailing of the first panel; when in place each panel should be anchored by at least 12 nails.

Continue adding and interlocking the panels, working across the base of the wall. Then add panels in parallel rows across the wall until you reach the desired height.

At the end of a row, if the panel does not fit exactly, measure the space remaining. Mark and score the back of the panel board to fit this measurement, and cut through the board with a utility knife along the scored line. Pry off unwanted bricks or break the bricks along the cut with a hammer and chisel.

4 **Filling the gaps.** Use the adhesive recommended by the manufacturer to fasten individual bricks over corner framing and into the spaces in the adjacent panel boards. To cover an outside corner, use L-shaped corner bricks; elsewhere, use flat bricks cut to size. To provide support for corner bricks until the adhesive sets (about 72 hours), drive finishing nails partway into the panel board just beneath each brick. After the adhesive has set, remove the nails and fill the mortar joints as shown in Steps 1 and 2, page 52.

Installing Plastic or Plaster Bricks

For many situations, lightweight, low-cost, fire-resistant imitation bricks of plastic or plaster-based compounds are almost as realistic as veneer bricks of kiln-fired clay. The best of these simulated bricks are roughly the same thickness as veneer bricks, and so near a match in color and texture that only by touching them can you tell they are not clay.

Like veneer bricks, the imitation bricks come in individual brick-sized facings and in specially shaped elements combining two or more brick faces—top and side; side and end; top, side and end—for turning edges and capping corners.

Imitation bricks are, however, easier than veneer bricks to install. They can be cut with a utility knife, and since the adhesive used to mount them has a mortar-like texture and color, there is no need for filling joints. The adhesive remains tacky for 10 to 30 minutes, long enough to make adjustments, and it sets completely in 60 minutes. The timing and tools for different adhesives may vary; follow the manufacturer's instructions.

1 Establishing the pattern. Using a 3-inch putty knife or notched trowel, spread the adhesive ¹⁄₁₆ inch thick down an inside corner, covering an area roughly brick-width. Starting at the top of the wall, set bricks down one side of the corner. Alternate full and half lengths—headers and stretchers—from row to row, for a running-bond pattern, as shown here. For a stacked pattern, line up stretchers. If you are working on an outside corner, set L-shaped corner bricks down the outside edge, alternating or stacking the long and short legs.

To attach each brick, coat the back with additional adhesive, then press the brick against the wall until the adhesive squeezes out around the edges of the brick. To seal the edges, smooth the adhesive with a dowel or a mason's jointer.

2 Completing the wall. Starting at the top, spread adhesive over the wall from the corner bricks inward, covering an area 4 or 5 feet square. Tack a level string across the wall as a guide, and set bricks in the chosen pattern, following the same mounting techniques used in Step 1. Repeat, coating additional areas with adhesive, and setting up string guidelines as needed to keep the courses level. Use a utility knife to cut bricks to fit into the odd spaces.

Unveiling the Charm of Brick

Many houses built between the Civil War and 1940 have masonry walls, usually of brick, with the inside surfaces covered by a layer of plaster. In many cases, by simply stripping away this layer, you can expose the inner brick wall to add color, texture and rustic charm to a room.

The whole process involves only four steps: The plaster is removed, the mortar joints are patched with new mortar, then the wall is washed with acid and finally is coated with a sealer. But the process is very dusty and takes at least 10 days, for you must allow drying time between steps. So before you decide to expose a wall, remove about a square foot of plaster in a lower corner and inspect the brick beneath, to determine if its color, texture and pattern are pleasing enough to warrant the work.

Exposing an entire wall calls for some fairly extensive preliminary preparations. The work is so dusty that you should remove all furniture, wall hangings and rugs from the room, as well as the contents of any closets or cabinets. The edges of closet and cabinet doors should then be sealed with masking tape and, if possible, so should all doors leading to other parts of the house. If the area is difficult to seal off, you can erect a protective dust curtain by taping lightweight plastic sheets from ceiling to floor, overlapping them about 8 inches so the overlap can serve as a door. Be sure, however, to leave windows in the work area open for maximum ventilation.

Since you will be removing all the plaster on the wall, including what lies behind the covers of electric outlets and light switches, you must turn off the electric circuits supplying current to them. This also prevents accidents involving electric wires that may be buried in the plaster. In addition, remove baseboards and other wood trim along the wall except the doorframes and window frames; these are generally left intact unless you plan to trim the jambs so that they match the exposed wall.

To protect the floor, cover it with a polyethylene drop sheet at least 4 mils thick. Only polyethylene this heavy will resist the acid wash, the plaster debris, and the constant foot traffic involved in the work and cleanup. The sheet should be anchored to the bottoms of the walls with industrial duct tape to prevent any dust or acid from creeping beneath it and marring the finish on the floors.

Probably the exposed mortar joints will require patching with new mortar. In many old houses, the original mortar contained, as a binder, horse hair—easily recognizable in the mortar's stringy edges. To patch such mortar, you will have to combine ordinary portland cement with a special calcium chloride bonding agent that is available at hardware stores under several commercial names. While you are patching the mortar, you may also have to conceal any wires that have been exposed, and deepen pockets for outlets or switches so they will be flush with the brick after the plaster has been removed.

If the bricks have been marred by lime in the plaster and mortar, which leaves white stains, you may want to brush the exposed wall with muriatic acid, a standard mason's wash available at paint stores. Muriatic acid removes many stains, old or new, but it must be handled with extreme care; it is diluted hydrochloric acid. Mix with water exactly as directed on the label, make sure there is proper ventilation and always wear a respirator, goggles and rubber gloves (not cloth or plastic ones).

If any skin is burned by the acid, first flush it with water, then apply a burn ointment. Throughout every step of the process be on the lookout for a stinging sensation in your nose or eyes; if you feel this, leave the room immediately and wash your eyes or nose thoroughly with water. Take a rest from the work until the stinging subsides.

Almost any old brick wall tends to powder, depositing a constant film of dust on its surroundings. To halt this, the wall can be coated with a sealer—usually latex or silicone. Satin-finish sealers are popular because they are invisible when dry, but wax-based sealers—though always somewhat glossy—are widely used in kitchens and bathrooms because they are easily cleaned.

1 Breaking away plaster. Wearing a respirator and goggles and using an 18-ounce bricklayer's hammer, work from the bottom of the wall to the top to break away the plaster. Hold the hammer so that its head strikes the surface at a 45° angle and strike each hammer blow about 6 inches above the existing break. This ensures smooth removal of the plaster in manageable chunks, and it protects the soft brick beneath from head-on hammer blows. Use the chisel end of the hammer to chip off stubborn clumps of plaster and to pry plaster out of tight spots, as in corners and under doorframes and window frames. If the plaster has been laid over metal or wood lath, wear gloves to pull the lath off.

2 **Scouring the brick surface.** Use a wire brush with medium-length bristles to remove stubborn plaster and loose mortar. Scrub hard enough to score each brick so that the acid and sealer will penetrate sufficiently.

Using ready-mixed mortar to which only water is added, repoint mortar joints, patch holes and fill in spaces around doorframes and window frames. To match old mortar, add sand to the new mortar to soften its color, following the manufacturer's advice. You can roughen the texture of the new mortar by dabbing at it with a stiff-bristled brush.

Wherever necessary use the chisel end of the bricklayer's hammer to deepen a recess for an electric outlet or switch. If any wires have been exposed by the removal of the plaster, clear out mortar joints to a depth of 1 inch in a stepped path leading to the outlet or switch box. If the wires are cloth-covered, slip a narrow, flexible metal conduit over them and fit them into the opened mortar joints, making sure to leave enough wire for the final connection at the box. Cover the cable with mortar.

Allow the new mortar to set for at least 48 hours before beginning the acid wash.

3 **Washing the wall with muriatic acid.** With windows wide open and wearing protective rubber gloves, goggles and a respirator, pour 1 part muriatic acid into a plastic bucket that already contains the recommended ratio of water. Apply this mixture to the wall with a stiff-bristled work brush, brushing in all directions but keeping spattering to a minimum. If acid begins to puddle anywhere on the polyethylene drop sheet, spread enough newspapers to absorb it. After washing the wall, rinse it by scrubbing it twice with clear water. Allow the wall to dry for at least a week before installing electrical outlets and switches and applying the sealer.

4 **Rewiring and sealing the wall.** Mortar all surfaces inside the pockets for electrical outlets and switches that will be flush with the brick wall. Slip the supply wire through the back of the fixture's box and push the unit into its pocket. Scrape away any excess mortar, then press a board flat against the box to smooth the mortar and to set the box flush with the wall. Let the mortar dry for 48 hours.

Brush a coat of latex or silicone-based sealer over the entire wall. When the sealer is dry, reconnect wires, replace the cover plates over outlets or switches and restore baseboards and any other wood trim that was removed, refitting them at the corners if necessary. If an outlet was originally in a baseboard, apply the sealer and, when it has dried, replace the baseboard, its outlet box and the cover plate.

5 **Caulking joints and gaps.** Fill a caulking gun with a compound to match the type of sealer used —either latex or silicone. Caulk all obvious joints and unsightly gaps, such as a break between adjoining sections of brick and plaster wall, and small gaps around doorframes and window frames. You can also caulk the crack between the top of a baseboard and the brick wall.

Lightweight Wall Panels to Divide and Decorate

Building a wall need not always be a major construction project involving extensive measuring, sawing, leveling and hammering. It is perfectly possible to separate one area of a room from another, or even to create an entirely new room, with a lightweight room divider that assembles with a minimum of fuss.

Such a divider wall can consist of rigid panels set in a wood frame, or of wallboard fastened to a metal-stud frame. Metal studs, long used for speedy and economical partitioning of offices, are now available in kit form for residential use. So, for that matter, are wood-framed dividers, but the framing is so simple that it is just about as easy to build your own.

The choice of panel materials for a wood-framed divider is almost unlimited. There are rigid plastic sheets in a rainbow of colors and varying degrees of transparency, from clear to opaque. Wire mesh and perforated metal, sold in sheets, also come in a range of colors and patterns, as does perforated hardboard. Sheets of rigid plastic foam have the added advantage of muffling sound, but they are fragile and should not be used for a divider that may get rough handling.

At somewhat higher prices there is a choice of caning or woven wood, both of which come in strips or sheets; and mirror or glass, which are sold in sheet or tiles. If you use sheet glass, buy the sturdier safety or tempered variety. Many artisan metalworkers and blacksmiths will design and make iron grillwork for mounting in frames, or you can even fill the frame with a quilt or a hand-loomed rug, hung between two poles. For an outstanding design at low cost, it would be hard to beat a divider wall of chicken wire supporting a vigorous growth of English ivy or climbing philodendron.

The framing materials used and the methods of joining them will depend somewhat on the panel choice, although personal preference is the main factor. The frames shown here are for light, thin panel materials like plastic or tempered hardboard, and are built from 1-by-3s. For heavier panels you might use 2-by-3, 2-by-4 or even 4-by-4 posts.

In the basic divider illustrated, for panels not more than ¼ inch thick, the edge of the panel is sandwiched between a continuous strip of lattice attached to one side of the frame, and a continuous strip of quarter-round molding. This makes a delicate divider but one that is different on its two sides. For panels thicker than ¼ inch, set in thicker frames, it is customary to use quarter-round molding on both sides, resulting in a stronger but bulkier divider whose two sides are identical.

The height of the frame depends on whether you want a full floor-to-ceiling divider or one with open spaces at the top and bottom. If you elect to make a full-length divider, the frame should actually be ¼ inch shorter than the floor-to-ceiling measurement, so that its edge will not catch against the ceiling when you are raising the divider into place. For similar ease in slipping the panels into the frame, make the inside width of the frame ⅛ inch wider than the panel.

Four types of divider walls. Wood-framed divider walls can take four basic forms, giving various degrees of privacy. One is a single rectangle extending from floor to ceiling (*top left*); another, with air space above and below, is mounted in an H-shaped frame (*top right*). Either can be used in multiples to stretch farther or to accommodate narrow panels (*bottom left*). Finally, a panel can be floated on wires between the ceiling and the floor (*bottom right*).

Building a Divider Frame

1 **Constructing the frame.** Fasten corners of the frame with wood glue and finishing nails, using either mitered joints or butt joints, depending on the design of the frame (butt joints are used for H frames). For a mitered corner, cut the 1-by-3s to 45° angles and apply glue to the mitered edges; fasten them together with a corner clamp, then drive finishing nails into the joint from both directions. For a butt joint, apply glue and toenail the joint (*inset*).

Scribe a guideline around the back of the frame, 7⁄8 inch in from the inner edge. Miter and cut four 1¾-inch lattice strips so their outer edges are the same length as the scribed lines.

CORNER CLAMP

2 **Tacking lattice to the frame.** Apply wood glue to the back of the frame, between the inner edge and the scribed line. Lay the lattice strips against the frame so that they align with the scribed line and extend 7⁄8 inch beyond the inner edge of the frame. Fasten the lattice to the frame with ¾-inch brads, spaced 6 inches apart. Then turn the frame right side up and slide the panel in, resting it on the lattice strips.

3 Securing the panel. Measure and miter four lengths of ½-inch quarter-round molding, or other similar trim, to fit the inside edges of the frame. Set each piece of trim against the panel and fasten it to the frame edge with glue and brads driven at an angle *(left inset)*.

If the panel is more than ¼ inch thick and the frame more than ¾ inch thick, do not use lattice strips to secure the panel. Instead, fasten the panel into the frame with quarter-round molding on both sides *(right inset)*.

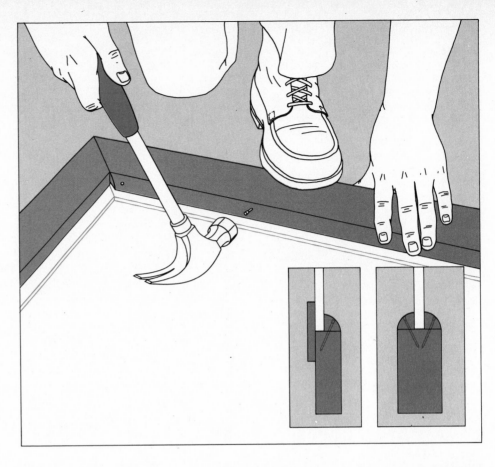

Extending a Divider with Lattice Strips

Connecting divider panels. To join two framed panels, butt their sides together and cover the joint with a lattice strip lapped equally over both frames. Make the strip the same length as the lattice panel supports. Fasten in place with glue and ¾-inch brads, spaced 6 inches apart. Then turn the frame over and fasten an identical strip of lattice to the other side.

Alternatively, set two or more panels into a single frame *(page 58, bottom left)*, by dividing a large frame with vertical 1-by-3s. Fasten the verticals to the frame with butt joints.

Three Ways of Erecting Dividers

Hanging a floating frame. If your divider frame lines up with a ceiling joist, turn two eye screws into the joist; otherwise use toggles or expansion shields to fasten two eyebolts to the ceiling. Fasten corresponding eye screws to the panel frame, and hang the frame with picture wire; make the two wires the same length. Fasten eye screws to the floor beneath the frame and connect these to eye screws in the frame.

Bracing an H frame. Hold the divider in place and mark guidelines on the ceiling for two angle-iron braces; then fasten angle irons against the ceiling, using expansion shields in plaster, flathead toggle bolts in wallboard. Raise the divider into place and attach the free leg of the angle iron to the frame *(inset)*. Check the panel with a level to make sure it is plumb, then toenail the bottom of the frame to the floor.

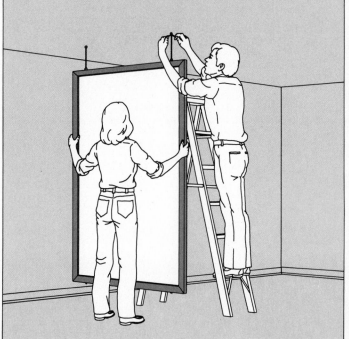 

Bracketing a solid frame. Glue and nail a length of decorative molding, mitered at one end, to the ceiling. Make sure the lower edge of the molding equals the width of the divider frame and is mitered so the molding pattern is upside down *(page 80)*—opposite to the position it would occupy if used at the floor. Raise the divider against the molding, and nail through the molding and into the divider frame. Attach an identical length of molding to the opposite side of the divider, then finish the exposed end of the divider with a short section of molding, mitered at both ends *(inset)*. (To make the divider fit snugly against the wall, either notch the baseboard and its shoe molding or scribe and notch the corner of the divider frame.)

Secure the divider to the floor with nails or screws, toenailed through the frame. Alternatively, bracket the bottom of the divider with the same molding arrangement used at the top, but cut in reverse, with the pattern right side up.

Metal Framing: A Snap to Install

Sturdier than a wall divider but quicker and easier to install than a wall framed with wood 2-by-4s, a metal-stud wall is convenient for enclosing the laundry area of a basement, for example, or for creating a privacy partition in a bedroom shared by children. Although the framing elements of a metal-stud wall are light enough to be cut with metal shears, the finished wall, when covered with gypsum wallboard, is as rigid as the same material supported by wood studs.

Metal framing is sold in kit form for short sections of wall, or can be purchased by the piece for larger installations; in that form it is available from many building-supply distributors. All systems consist of bracket-shaped studs and lighter-weight bracket-shaped tracks; the sides of the tracks angle slightly inward and the studs snap into them. The back of each stud, called its spine, is stiffened with ribbing and has holes to accommodate electrical or plumbing lines.

Metal framing goes up in the same sequence as wood framing. First, lengths of track—corresponding to the sole and top plates of a wood-framed wall—are measured, cut and fastened to the floor and ceiling. Then the studs, set 16 inches apart, are snapped into the tracks. Generally the studs are held in place by pressure, but if you plan to pull wires or pipes through them, fasten the stud ends to their tracks with sheet-metal screws.

To make an opening for a doorway, you simply construct an outer frame of metal studs for the inner frame of wood 2-by-4s; the door jambs will be attached to the wood studs just as they are in a wood-framed wall. To fasten wallboard to metal studs and tracks, follow the sequence shown on page 21, but use Type S dry-wall screws. These screws can be driven with a ¼- or ⅜-inch variable-speed drill fitted with a Phillips-head screwdriver bit or, more easily, with a rented power screw gun.

Framing a Partition Wall with Steel

1 Cutting the track. Use straight-cutting metal shears to trim tracks for the top and bottom plates. Cut flanges first, then the spine. When two sections of track meet at a corner (*left inset*), measure back on their inside flanges a distance equal to the inside width of the track. Cut the flanges there, then flatten them outward. Overlap the two sections of track. Where a wall intersects another (*right inset*), cut and flatten the inside flange of the intersected track and both flanges of the intersecting track. Overlap the two sections.

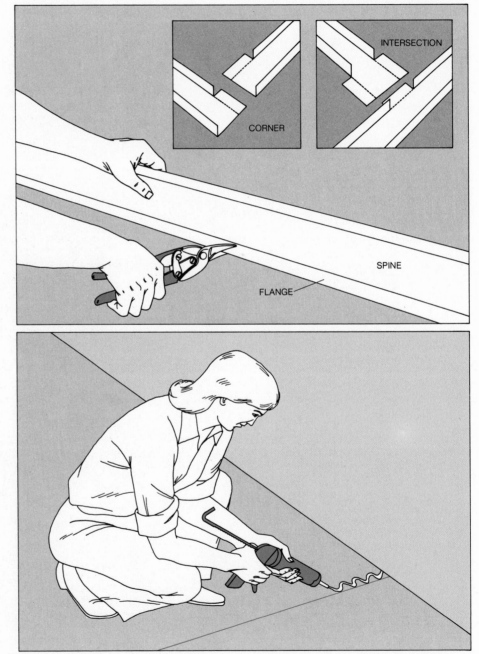

INTERSECTION

CORNER

SPINE

FLANGE

2 Laying the floor track. Snap a chalk line on the floor to mark the location of one edge of the track, then apply a ⅜-inch-wide bead of panel adhesive along the track side of the chalk line, laying down a serpentine pattern. Press the track firmly into the panel adhesive, making sure the edge of the track is aligned with the chalk line. If you prefer, omit the panel adhesive and fasten the track to a concrete floor with fluted masonry nails, or to a wood floor with sheet-metal screws or spiral nails. Space the screws or nails 2 feet apart.

3 **Fastening the ceiling track.** Use a plumb bob to mark three or more points on the ceiling directly above the floor track, align the ceiling track with these points and fasten it in place. If the track runs across joists or runs along the length of one joist, use sheet-metal screws or spiral nails to fasten the track in place. If the track runs parallel to and between joists, and the ceiling is already in place, use Molly bolts as fasteners. If the ceiling is unfinished and the track runs between joists, nail wood blocks between those joists at 2-foot intervals and use the blocks as a support for fastening the track.

4 **Erecting the studs.** Cut studs ¼ inch shorter than the height of the new wall, and snap each stud into place by setting it edgewise into the floor and ceiling tracks, then twisting it. Set the first stud 2 inches out from the existing wall, to allow room for working with a power drill or screw gun when you attach the wallboard. Place succeeding studs so that their centers are 16 inches apart. Use a level to plumb each stud.

Making Way for a Door

Building a frame-within-a-frame. To construct a support for a door's rough frame of 2-by-4s, first determine the size of the opening required for the rough frame and erect two metal studs for it. Space the studs 3 inches farther apart than the width needed for the rough opening, and face their spines toward the opening. Join the studs with a header made from a piece of track 12 inches longer than the width needed for the opening. To shape the header, cut the flanges at a 45° angle, 6 inches in from each end and slanted toward the ends of the header (*inset*). Bend down the 6-inch ends into right angles and fasten them to the metal studs with sheet-metal screws, setting the header 1½ inches above the height necessary for the opening.

Add an interior frame of 2-by-4s, attaching them to the metal frame with sheet-metal screws at 2-foot intervals. Cut a cripple stud—a short section—to fit between the header and the ceiling track at the center of the opening. Snap it into place as you would a full-length stud.

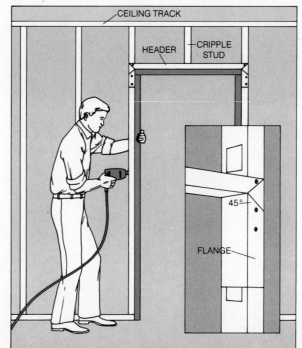

Installing Boxes, Wires and Pipes

Installing an electrical box. An electrical box that has flanges on one side is the easiest type to install in a new metal-stud wall. To mount the flanges on a stud, position the face of the box so that it will be flush with the wall surface; then drill pilot holes into the metal stud and secure the box with sheet-metal screws.

Running cable through metal studs. Use plastic grommets, available at electrical-supply stores, to protect the electrical cable from the sharp sheet-metal edges of the stud holes. Snap the grommets into the holes at the appropriate height, then pass the cable through the grommet-rimmed openings to the electrical box.

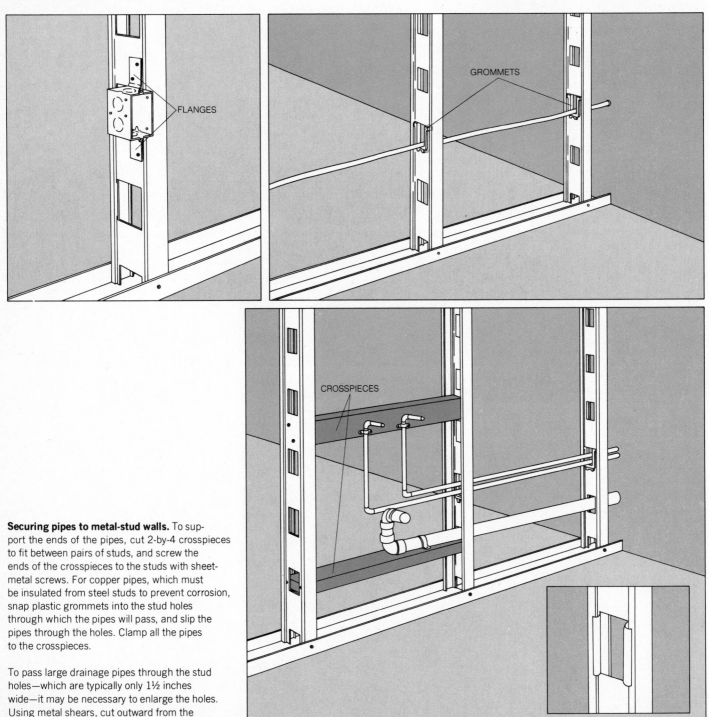

FLANGES

GROMMETS

CROSSPIECES

Securing pipes to metal-stud walls. To support the ends of the pipes, cut 2-by-4 crosspieces to fit between pairs of studs, and screw the ends of the crosspieces to the studs with sheet-metal screws. For copper pipes, which must be insulated from steel studs to prevent corrosion, snap plastic grommets into the stud holes through which the pipes will pass, and slip the pipes through the holes. Clamp all the pipes to the crosspieces.

To pass large drainage pipes through the stud holes—which are typically only 1½ inches wide—it may be necessary to enlarge the holes. Using metal shears, cut outward from the holes (inset) and bend the metal edges back.

The Old Tin Ceiling Makes a Comeback

The quaint tin ceiling, which may have graced your grandparents' favorite ice-cream parlor with its classical harps and gargoyled lion heads, is back. Indestructible, and a uniquely American record of the eclectic ornamental styles of the 19th and early 20th Centuries, metal was the second most popular ceiling material, after plaster, until it practically disappeared in the 1930s. It is now staging a comeback in the homes of collectors and interior designers. Even in its heyday—1895 to 1915—the tin ceiling did not enjoy such attention.

Originally invented around 1868 as an inexpensive way to hide bad plaster, the tin ceiling soon proved to be superior to plaster in nearly every respect, especially as a firestop. Tests showed that a tin ceiling could withstand a temperature of 1,369° for an hour and 10 minutes, whereas plaster collapsed in 12 minutes. There were actual cases in which the metal on a first-floor ceiling kept a fire from spreading to upper stories of a building, though the first floor was destroyed; metal even saved a room surrounded by a full-scale conflagration. Thus it became the material of choice for the ceilings of theaters, restaurants and other commercial buildings regulated by strict fire codes.

Tin ceilings graced very few private homes, however, though they were occasionally found in hallways and bathrooms. More often, homeowners used the stamped designs as dados—the decorated lower part of a wall—and some dado patterns came with a metal chair rail molded into the design. There were also wall plates as much as 8 feet tall, making it possible to envelop an entire room in decorative metal. But the public never liked metal as much as plaster, and with the advent of acoustic tile and gypsum wallboard, tin walls and ceilings suddenly became as passé as knickers and spittoons.

A revived interest in memorabilia changed all that, and fortunately, two of the original manufacturers—W. F. Norman of Nevada, Missouri, and the Barney Brainum-Shanker Steel Company of Glendale, New York—had kept their old dies and presses. Their patterns, some of which are shown in the photographs below, include Greek, Oriental, Romanesque, colonial, rococo, Gothic, Empire and Art-Deco motifs.

The patterns come stamped as they were in Teddy Roosevelt's day, on thin sheets of steel or copper; few tin ceilings were actually tin. (The Norman company does its stamping with antique rope-drop hammers based on 17th Century French equipment, operated by shafts and pulleys. Barney Brainum-Shanker Steel stamps its plates one at a time on a Gargantuan two-story power press built in 1928.)

The method of installation, like the sheets themselves, has not changed. The main ceiling pieces, which come in sheets of various dimensions—1-by-1, 1-by-2, 2-by-4 or 2-by-8—are tacked to furring strips spaced 12 inches on center. Borders, center medallions and cornice pieces are added later, and so are wainscoting pieces for the walls.

Motifs in pressed metal. These interchangeable tin-ceiling patterns can be mixed and matched to suit any taste, from Classical to Art Deco. The squares embellish the main ceiling; the narrower outside patterns combine three separate pieces—cornice, filler and border—to mate the ceiling to the wall.

3

The Richness of Wood Paneling

Paneling with solid boards. Tongue-and-groove edges ease the task of paneling with solid-wood boards. Nails are driven diagonally through the tongue to anchor each board to furring strips, and the nailheads are then hidden from view by the grooved edge of the next board. Fluting carved in the boards creates patterns of light and shadow across the finished wall.

It is somehow appropriate that wood paneling should be a favorite American material for covering walls. Ever since the first settlers arrived, to find a continent thick with virgin forests, Americans have seen wood as one of their greatest natural resources. By 1610 the colonists were exporting many fine woods back to Europe, and the earliest Revolutionary flag bore the likeness of a white pine tree.

The early use of wood paneling in American homes was part of the inevitable response to such abundance. As they cleared the land, Americans used the trees they felled for everything—fences, firewood, furniture, tools, structural timbers and the finished walls of houses. As makeshift rusticity matured into civilized prosperity, the craftsmanship of wood likewise became more refined.

To create the intricate paneling and wainscoting that graced many colonial homes, cabinetmakers worked each board by hand, carving the precise joints as well as the elaborate surface designs. As late as 1900, it was not unusual for a city like San Francisco to order an entire fleet of new streetcars with interiors of finely worked cherry paneling. But soon afterward the use of wood paneling went into decline—as Americans began to run short of both time and trees.

Fortunately for modern homeowners, technology has come to the rescue, solving, to a great degree, both problems. The modern lumber mill has reduced the amount of money and expertise required to obtain solid-wood paneling. Nowadays solid boards are machine-milled rather than hand-shaped, and come with a variety of edge joints that permit them to be installed vertically, horizontally or diagonally. And the fancy carving of decorative raised panels can now be done mechanically, and in a matter of minutes.

In addition, the development of plywood has made wood paneling more accessible to more people. Widely available in standard 4-foot-by-8-foot sizes, plywood paneling consists of several thin layers of wood glued together, the outermost layer a veneer of fine wood. Special blades shave these veneers as thin as $1/28$ inch, in long sheets that unroll like paper towels from logs spinning on lathes. A single large tree can yield as much as 90,000 square feet of veneer. Less expensive than solid wood and easier to install, these mass-produced panels are much prized by time- and cost-conscious consumers.

For convenience and versatility, no mass-produced wood paneling can beat hardboard—a tough, pliable, water-resistant material made from wood fibers. Hardboard is manufactured in a variety of colors and textures; much of it is covered with a paper or vinyl photograph of a material such as wicker, marble, brick—or wood. Thus, though the virgin forests are sadly depleted, substitutes abound—and no home need be without the warmth and elegance of wood.

Covering Walls with Large Sheets of Wood Veneer

Nothing else brings the warmth and elegance of wood to a room as quickly and effectively as veneer paneling for the walls. Available in hundreds of styles, wood-veneer panels are far less costly than solid-wood boards *(page 82)* and even easier to install than gypsum wallboard *(page 18)*. Vertical joints can be disguised by an incised pattern on the panels, and other edges hidden by special moldings. The panels are attached to a framework of studs or furring strips *(pages 11-17)* just as wallboard is or, even better, to wallboard itself.

Yet, for all its advantages, paneling also has several disadvantages that have limited its use to certain rooms, such as recreation rooms and dens. It is more expensive than wallboard and, because of its construction, it is more flammable and more vulnerable to damage.

Typically, veneer paneling is a backing of plywood or particleboard veneered in one of several ways—with a thin layer of fine wood, with a thin sheet of less desirable wood *(chart, opposite)*, or with a simulated wood grain printed on paper or vinyl. The panels come in sheets $\frac{5}{32}$, $\frac{3}{16}$ or ¼ inch thick, and this thinness, along with the materials used, makes them the least fire-resistant of all common wall surfaces. National fire-testing laboratories give most veneer panels the same poor flame-spread rating, Class C or its equivalent, FS-200—ratings you should find stamped on each panel back.

Fire-prevention experts warn against putting large expanses of veneer paneling directly over wall studs or furring strips, particularly in such fire-prone areas as halls, stairways, kitchens and utility rooms. Instead, they recommend that you either apply panels directly to an existing wall of gypsum or plaster, or cover any stud wall or furring framework with ½-inch wallboard. When you apply the panels, avoid placing wallboard joints and panel joints along the same studs. The wallboard underlayer not only multiplies the wall's fire resistance ninefold, to a far safer level, but also triples its resistance to impact and increases sound absorption by 43 per cent.

All veneer panels come in sheets 4 feet by 8 feet, and some are available as tall as 12 feet—but the latter are expensive, and 8-foot sheets should suffice to cover the loftiest wall *(page 79)*. Both the real-wood veneers and the printed-wood panels are made in a variety of colors and grains, and most styles have a vertical-groove pattern that makes them look like boards. The spacing between grooves is designed to seem random, but in fact a groove always falls at or near a 16- or a 24-inch interval, to make it easy to find the studs or furring strips when you are fastening the panels. At the edges, vertical half-grooves disguise joints.

To estimate how many panels you will need to cover an area, measure the total width of the walls in feet, and divide by 4. Some suppliers recommend that you then subtract one half panel for a door and one quarter panel for a window, on the assumption that pieces cut from window and door panels can be used elsewhere, but in practice they are not likely to fit anywhere else.

After you buy the panels, store them in the room where they will be used, stacked one atop another with small wood blocks between. Give them 48 hours to adjust to the temperature and humidity of the room; this will reduce the danger of shrinkage or expansion after the panels are installed. Next, if the panels have a real-wood veneer with truly random graining, stand them against the wall and arrange them to suit your taste. A few panels may have a stronger grain than others, a few may be lighter or darker, or the horizontal joints of the core may show in some grooves. Printed panels, which are flawless and nearly identical, can go up in any order.

You can cut plywood veneer panels with a handsaw or power saw. For long straight cuts, most carpenters prefer a portable circular saw fitted with a special plywood blade that has six teeth per inch. For short straight cuts and curved cuts, use a saber saw with 10 teeth per inch. The chief advantage of circular and saber saws is that they cut on the upstroke; this enables you to mark your cutting lines on the back of the panel and confine most of the splinters from the cut to that surface. With any other type of saw, including a radial-arm or table saw, you will have to control splinters by marking the finished side of the panel and cutting with that side facing up.

How you fasten panels to a wall depends on whether you plan to remove them in the future. The choices are nails alone, or nails used with panel adhesive. Applying panel adhesive, which goes on studs or furring strips in a bead from a caulking gun, is faster and easier than hammering in the many nails needed if nails alone are to hold the panels. But glued panels are much harder to salvage.

If you elect to use adhesive, buy one 11-ounce tube for every three panels. As for nails, buy special paneling brads, colored to match the panels, sold by panel suppliers. To fasten panels directly to studs or furring strips, use 1-inch nails; when you also nail through wallboard or plaster, use 1⅝-inch nails.

Once in place, paneling requires almost no attention beyond an occasional wiping with a damp cloth and mild detergent. Scratches cannot be removed, but they can be concealed with matching wood stain. If they are no deeper than the finish layer of the panel, you may be able to hide them by rubbing clear wax into them with a damp cloth. For concealing deep mars, some manufacturers offer putty sticks in colors that match their panels. Over the years, some panels fade when exposed to light and air, leaving unfaded areas behind pictures that were hung flat against the wall. To prevent this—or to soften the line between faded and unfaded areas—stick push pins or tacks into the backs of picture frames, creating a ½-inch air space behind them.

Four Basic Variations in Wall Panels

Choosing a panel. Use the chart below to help you choose paneling that suits your needs. Listed vertically are four panel types; listed horizontally are their characteristics. All of the panels are composite to some extent, composed of wood particles, wood fibers or plywood. Also, the four categories are not mutually exclusive. Some manufacturers of plywood veneer panels use par-

ticleboard instead of plywood for the core, for example; some enhance the appearance of plywood veneer panels by printing additional wood grain over the grain already present. Whether the grain pattern on a panel is simulated photographically or the real thing may be unimportant to you if it is convincing; thinness will not matter if the panels are applied over wallboard.

Panel	Composition	Advantages	Disadvantages
Simulated pattern on particleboard	Compressed and glued wood particles covered with a paper-, vinyl- or wood-printed finish; $3/16$ inch thick	Most economical	Weak, rigid and brittle; does not hold nails well; dulls saw blades quickly
Simulated pattern on hardboard	Heated and compressed wood-fiber covered with paper- or wood-printed finish; $5/32$ or $3/16$ inch thick	Great variety of styles; can simulate brick, stucco or marble as well as wood; stronger than particleboard	Dulls saw blades quickly
Simulated pattern on plywood	Plywood covered with a paper-, vinyl- or wood-printed finish; $5/32$ or $3/16$ inch thick	Stronger and more flexible than particleboard or hardboard; more economical than plywood veneered with real wood. Can be bent to fit curved walls.	Splinters easily; usually thinner and less solid than real wood veneer
Wood veneer on plywood	Real wood veneer over a plywood backing. Veneer can be hardwood or softwood, ranging in quality from inexpensive pine to rosewood. Surface is protected by a clear or slightly tinted plastic coating. Usually ¼ inch thick	Texture and patina of real wood; best resistance to moisture, sound and impact. Each panel is unique.	Two to four times as expensive as printed panels; splinters easily

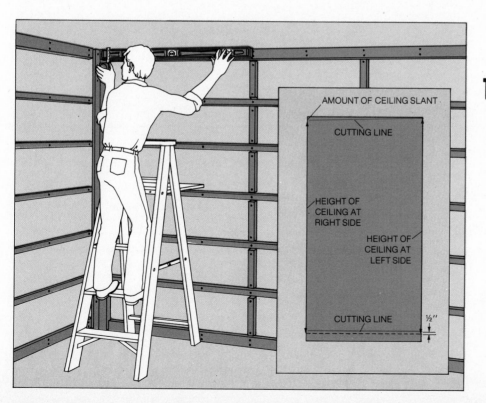

Fitting and Cutting Panels to Cover a Wall

1 **Establishing cutting lines.** At either an inside or an outside corner of the room, hold a 4-foot level against the top of the wall to check whether the ceiling slants. If it does, measure the gap between the level and the ceiling at the ceiling's highest point. Measure this distance down one side of the panel and draw a line from that point to the opposite corner of the panel (*inset*). If you are using a circular saw or saber saw, mark the cutting line on the back of the panel; for any other type of saw, mark on the front.

Measure the distance from floor to ceiling at the corner of the room and 4 feet away from the corner, along the wall. Subtract ½ inch from both measurements and mark these distances down the corresponding sides of the panel, measuring from the top cutting line or from the actual top of the panel, depending on whether the ceiling slopes. Draw a bottom cutting line across the panel between the marks.

AMOUNT OF CEILING SLANT

CUTTING LINE

HEIGHT OF CEILING AT RIGHT SIDE

HEIGHT OF CEILING AT LEFT SIDE

CUTTING LINE   ½"

2 Sawing the panels. If you use a portable circular saw to trim the panel, measure the distance from the left side of the saw blade to the left side of the base plate and clamp a straight-edged piece of wood to the panel, at this distance from the cutting line. Use the straight edge as a guide while you cut the panel.

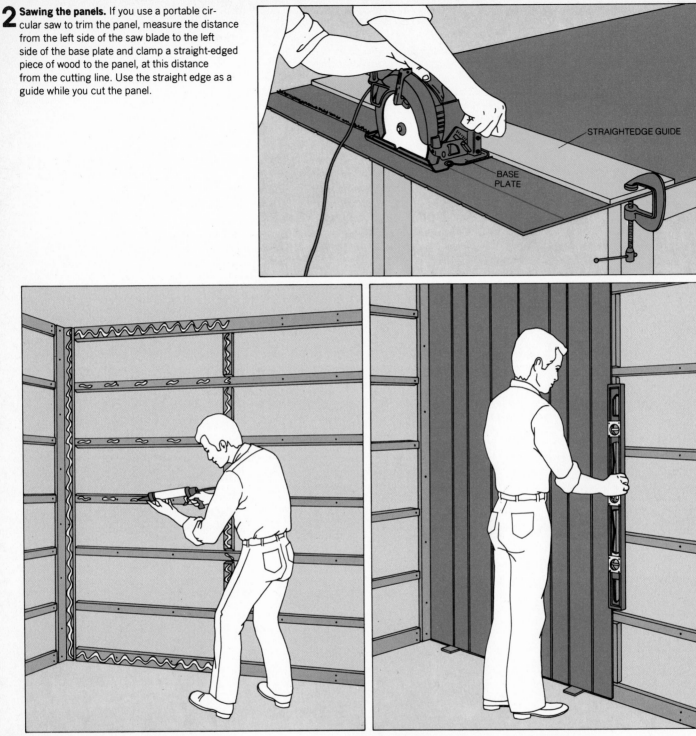

STRAIGHTEDGE GUIDE

BASE PLATE

3 Applying panel adhesive. If you are using panel adhesive, apply it in a continuous ⅛-inch-wide serpentine bead to all the studs, furring strips or wall surfaces that will underlie panel edges. On intermediate studs or furring strips, apply the adhesive in 3-inch-long beads 6 inches apart; on a solid wall surface, apply intermediate rows of adhesive in continuous vertical lines about 16 inches apart. You may want to measure and mark these lines with pencil or chalk.

4 Plumbing the first panel. Place the panel in position and wedge shims beneath it to lift it ¼ inch off the floor. Using a 4-foot carpenter's level, plumb the panel's outer edge by having a helper adjust the shims. Do this carefully, because the eventual appearance of all the paneling, especially at the corners of the room, will depend on how vertical the grooves are in the first panel. Tack the panel in place temporarily with four panel nails along the top edge.

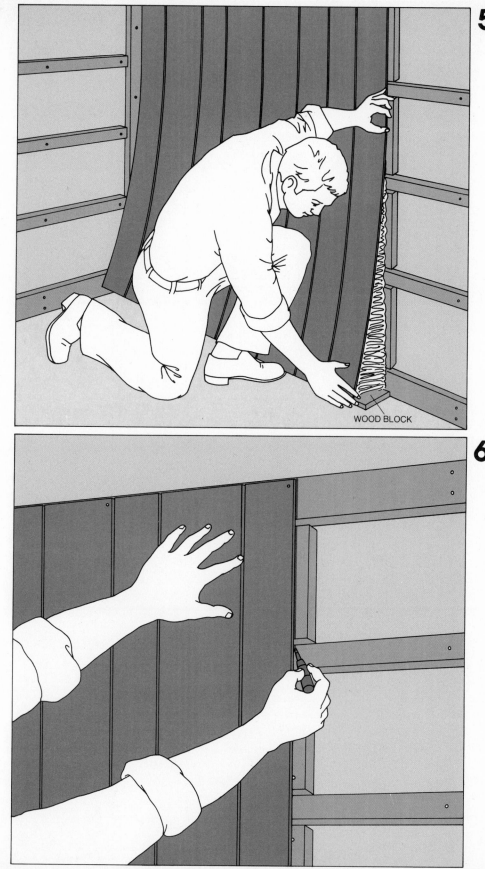

WOOD BLOCK

5 **Securing the panel.** Press the panel against the wall to compress the adhesive, then pull out the bottom of the panel and insert two 8-inch wood blocks between the panel and the wall, one at each side. Let the adhesive dry for the time the manufacturer recommends, then remove the blocks and push the panel against the wall again, tapping it with your fist to make a tight seal. Wipe away any adhesive on the finished face of the panel with a rag dipped in paint thinner. Nail the edges of the panel to the wall, spacing the nails 1 foot apart; then nail the panel to the wall along the intermediate studs or furring strips at 2-foot intervals, placing the nails either in the grooves or ⅛ inch from their edges. Set all panel nails with a nail set.

If you are not using panel adhesive, nail the panel to the wall every 8 inches along the edges, and every 12 inches along intermediate studs or furring strips. Again, set all nails with a nail set.

6 **Setting adjoining panels.** Before adding a second panel, run a felt-tip pen, the color of the grooves, along the edge of the panel just installed, staining the furring strip, stud or wall surface. This will keep the joint between panels inconspicuous, even if the panels shrink. Then install subsequent panels the same way as the first, plumbing each one by butting it against the edge of the last panel installed and trimming ends as necessary.

7 **Trimming a panel to fit a corner.** First cut the corner panel to the proper height (*Steps 1 and 2*), then determine its width by measuring the distance from the corner of the room to the edge of the last panel installed, at both ceiling and floor. Mark these distances on the top and bottom edges of the corner panel, positioning them so that the factory-cut edge of this panel will fall against the panel already in place. Snap a chalk line between the two marks and cut along the line. Install the cut panel as you would a full-width panel, shaving down the cut edge, if necessary, with a block plane so that the edge fits against the corner stud.

Continue to panel around the corner by installing the first panel of the next wall as in Steps 1 through 5, using a level to plumb the panel. If this wall is less than 4 feet wide—the width of one panel—trim the panel to fit, but be sure to use its factory-cut edge to plumb it.

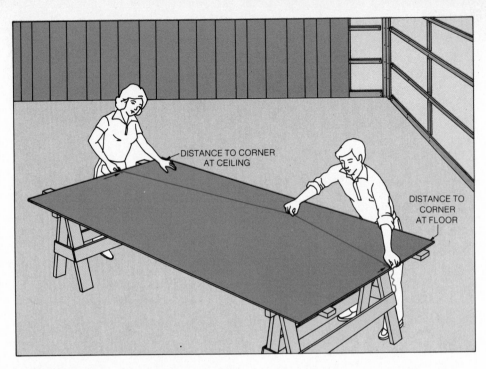

DISTANCE TO CORNER AT CEILING

DISTANCE TO CORNER AT FLOOR

Plotting the Curves to Fit Rounded Windows

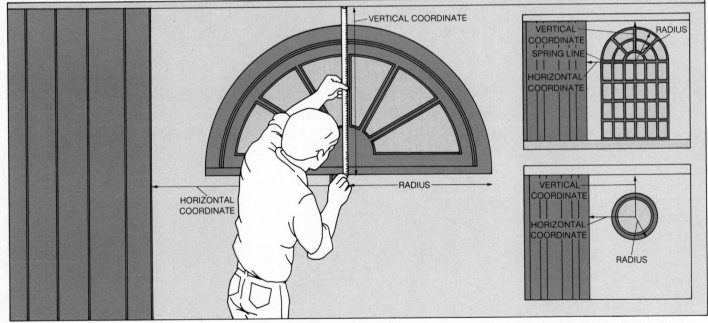

VERTICAL COORDINATE

HORIZONTAL COORDINATE

RADIUS

VERTICAL COORDINATE

RADIUS

SPRING LINE

HORIZONTAL COORDINATE

VERTICAL COORDINATE

HORIZONTAL COORDINATE

RADIUS

1 **Locating the center of the circle.** To fit a panel around a circular or semicircular window, remove the window moldings and find the geometric center of the basic circle. For a semicircular window, measure the distance from the ceiling to the bottom of the window frame; then measure from the center of the bottom of the frame to the edge of the last panel installed. Using these two distances as coordinates, and subtracting ¼ inch from the vertical measurement for ease in fitting the panel, plot the center of the base of the semicircle on the panel.

If the semicircle is an arch framing the top of a door or window that has straight sides, find the center of the base of the semicircle by first holding a straightedge along the inside edge of the window and noting the point where the frame begins to curve (*top inset*). Next, measure down to this point, known as the spring line, from the ceiling, and note this distance. Then measure the radius of the semicircle and to this add the distance from the spring line to the last panel installed. Use these vertical and horizontal coordinates, again subtracting ¼ inch from

the vertical measurement, to plot the center of the semicircle on the panel.

For a circular window, find the point on the window frame nearest to the last panel installed (*bottom inset*). Measure down to this point and subtract ¼ inch for the vertical clearance. Then measure the distance from this point to the edge of the last panel installed and to this distance add the radius of the circle. Use these vertical and horizontal coordinates, as above, to plot the center of the circle on the panel.

2 Drawing the curve. Tack a nail at the center point plotted on the panel, and tie one end of a string to the nail. Attach a pencil to the other end of the string at a distance equal to the radius of the semicircle or circle. Swing the pencil in an arc to duplicate the curve of the window frame. If the window cannot be covered by a single panel, lay two plumbed and trimmed panels side by side as you will install them and draw the window outline on the combined pair.

Finish the outline for a semicircular window or arched window by plotting the straight lines that continue from the curve. Cut out the curved section of the outline with a saber saw, and any straight sections with a circular saw.

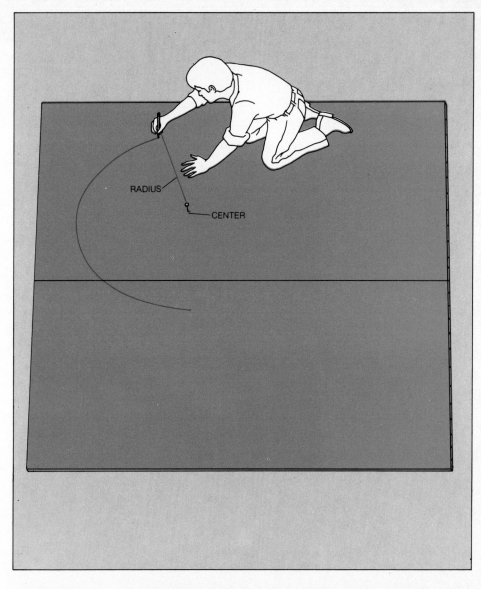

Matching Paneling to Odd-shaped Openings

Making grooves turn a corner. When paneling around a corner where one surface is horizontal, as at the bottom or top of a recessed window, align the grooves of the horizontal and vertical panel pieces where the two surfaces meet. For the horizontal panel, use the waste piece cut from the vertical panel, trimming it as needed to fit the space. To line up the grooves, measure the distance from a groove in the vertical panel to the side of the window opening, and match this distance on the horizontal panel, using the corresponding groove as a reference point.

Making a pattern for an irregular shape. Tape a large piece of paper over the opening, lining up one vertical edge of the paper with the edge of the last panel installed, and one horizontal edge of the paper with the ceiling line. Press the paper against the opening and outline the shape with a pencil. Remove the paper, cut out the marked area with scissors and use the remainder of the paper as a pattern. Position the pattern over the panel to be cut, aligning the vertical and horizontal edges of the paper with the appropriate panel edges, and mark the outline on the panel. Then cut and install the panel.

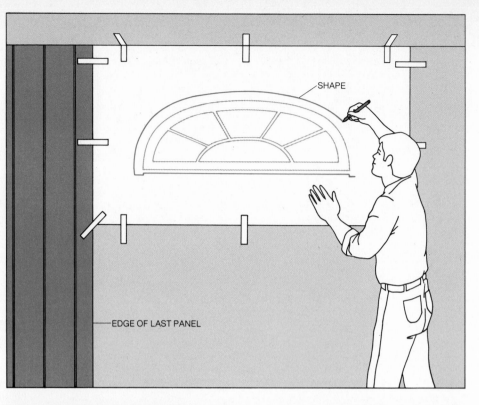

SHAPE

EDGE OF LAST PANEL

Making Way for Electric Boxes, Service Panels and Pipes

Marking for an electrical box. To mark the location of an electrical box on a section of paneling for a new wall, use the front edge of the box, which typically protrudes beyond the studs, for marking the cut. Rub the edge of the box with a piece of chalk (*left*), set the panel in its exact

position over the box, and strike the face of the panel with a padded woodblock to transfer the chalked outline onto the back of the panel (*right*). If the outline is not completely clear, use a spare electrical box as a pattern to fill in the missing sections with a pencil.

When you are paneling directly over an existing wall, a protruding switch or receptacle will prevent you from using the edges of the electrical box to mark the panel. Instead, you can plot the location of the box by the use of coordinates, as described on page 19.

Making a door for a service panel. Using the system of coordinates shown on page 19, transfer the location of the service panel to the back of the wood paneling and cut out the opening. Use the cutout section for a door, framing it with 1-by-2 strips glued to the back. If necessary, trim one long edge so that it will fit easily after hinges are mounted. Screw hinges onto the strips along one edge, set the door into its opening and screw the other wings of the hinges to one of the framing studs surrounding the service panel. Attach a knob to the front of a door, and a catch to the back and to a framing stud. For a more finished look, you can frame the opening with mitered molding (*inset*).

Perfect holes for protruding pipes. Using the system of coordinates shown on page 72, Step 1, establish the center of the pipe by measuring the distance from the outside of the pipe to the floor and to the last panel installed. Add half the pipe diameter to both measurements, then subtract ¼ inch from the vertical measurement, in order to allow that much clearance at the floor. Transfer these vertical and horizontal coordinates to the panel back, indenting the point where they meet.

Use a hole saw matching the pipe diameter to drill a hole at this point, drilling only until the twist bit of the saw (*inset*) breaks through the face of the panel. Remove the saw, turn the panel over and finish sawing the hole from the face side, so any splinters will be on the back of the panel.

A Custom Cut around Obstacles

Unlike the panels made to cover them, walls cannot always be divided neatly into flat rectangular 8-foot sections. Invariably you will have areas with odd shapes: the triangular section of wall above or below a staircase; the outsized walls beneath a cathedral ceiling; corners that dogleg around a brick or stone fireplace, or even corners that curve.

For all of these situations, you will need to mark and cut panels in special ways—sometimes diagonally, sometimes along curved or irregular lines. To cover oddly shaped seams and corners, you may need to cut special moldings.

Probably the most commonly encountered need for custom-cut paneling is found along stairways, where you must slice the panels to match the diagonal line of the stringer boards framing the steps. Above or below stairs, the stringer follows the slant determined by the width of the treads and height of the risers, the vertical boards between treads.

When the framing studs are exposed in new construction, you can simply trace the diagonal line of the stringer by placing the panel directly against the studs. More likely, you will need to lay the panel flat on the floor and transfer the stringer angle to it by measuring coordinates, using a framing square.

In most cases only one edge of a staircase panel is involved—the bottom edge of paneling above the stairs, the top edge below them. But sometimes, on banister walls, both top and bottom are cut at the same angle, forming a parallelogram-shaped panel. Alternatively, paneling above the stairs may end at a point matching the ceiling line of the room below, where it is capped with a special molding; or it may extend all the way to the ceiling of the stairwell.

If you choose to run the paneling to the ceiling, you will undoubtedly be working with a wall taller than your panels, and you have several options—all of which also apply to other outsized wall areas. You can buy extra-tall panels, but these are expensive. You can also leave a gap along the bottom of the paneling, to be covered by baseboard molding held in alignment with a hidden ¼-inch-thick spacer strip; but this extends the paneling only 2 or 3 inches at most.

A third option is to put up the panels horizontally, one atop the other, until they reach the ceiling, using strips of vertical molding to cover the joints between their ends. Conversely, you can stack the panels vertically, covering their end joints with strips of horizontal molding. A final option is to cut the panels and turn them 45°, creating a ceiling-high pattern of herringbone stripes.

To create the herringbone pattern, you simply cut vertically patterned panels at angles and mount them tilted. The method works with either evenly or randomly spaced grooves, but in tilting the panels you lose some width. The reassembled, taller panel pieces will be 34 inches wide, instead of 48; furring strips behind them must be spaced accordingly.

Fitting panels to a curved wall involves yet another kind of custom cutting. Here you must painstakingly make shallow grooves in the back of each panel at precise intervals, a process that woodworkers call kerfing. The panel then can be flexed backward to round a gentle curve. This works only with plywood-backed panels; neither particleboard nor hardboard will bend far without breaking. In fact, plywood panels in their thinnest form—only 5/32 inch thick—can be bent around a shallow curve without kerfing.

Fitting Panels to the Angles of a Staircase

1 Measuring the slant of the stringer. To calculate the angle of the staircase stringer—the board against which the panels must fit—measure the "unit of rise" and "unit of run." To find the unit of rise, measure the distance from the top of one stair tread to the top of the next tread above or below. To find the unit of run, measure the distance over the tread from the front of one riser to the front of the next riser; ignore the tread's rounded lip.

On the back of the panel to be installed, mark two intersecting lines to locate the point where the slant of the stringer begins (*point A*). The vertical line shows the distance above the floor; the horizontal line, the distance from the edge of the last panel installed. Draw a line through point A parallel to the bottom of the panel, across the entire width (*inset*).

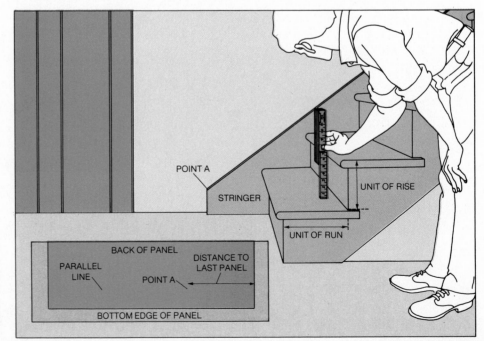

POINT A

STRINGER

UNIT OF RISE

UNIT OF RUN

BACK OF PANEL

PARALLEL LINE

DISTANCE TO LAST PANEL

POINT A

BOTTOM EDGE OF PANEL

2 **Marking the slant on the panel.** Place a framing square over the parallel line, with the apex of the square pointing toward the panel top. With the short leg of the square facing away from the panel edge that will join the last panel installed, adjust the square until the unit-of-run measurement, read on the outer scale of the long leg, rests at point A, while the unit-of-rise measurement, read on the outer edge of the short leg, intersects the parallel line. Draw a line along the long leg from point A to the apex of the square. Extend this line—which indicates the top edge of the stringer—across the panel.

Place the remaining panels to be installed face down alongside the first one, top edge and bottom edges even. Extend the slanted line across their backs until it crosses the top edge of a panel. Cut the panels along this line and along the line that runs from point A to the bottom of the panel. Install the panels (*inset*).

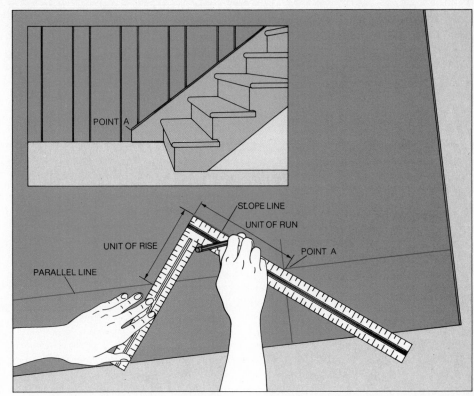

Making Panels Bend without Breaking

Kerfing a panel for bending. To bend a panel so it will cover a curved wall, make a series of shallow cuts in the back of the panel with a portable circular saw. Set the saw to cut ⅛ inch deep for a ¼-inch panel, 1/16 inch deep for a ³/16-inch panel. Support the entire panel, face down, on a solid worktable to prevent it from breaking and guide the saw with a straight piece of wood 8 feet long. Clamp the guide to the back of the panel, moving it for each cut. Space the kerfs about 1 inch apart, but take care not to place a kerf within 1 inch of a groove on the face of the panel. Kerf half the panel from one side of the worktable, starting at the edge and working to the center, then kerf the remaining half from the other side.

To test a section of kerfed panel, press it against the wall you intend to cover. If you feel strong resistance, space the kerfs at ½-inch intervals.

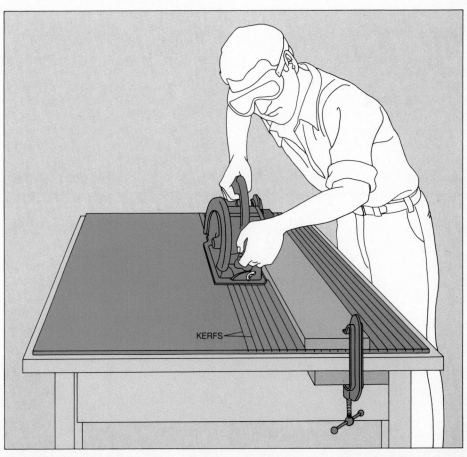

Contouring a Panel Edge
to Fit an Irregular Shape

1 **Measuring for the rough cutout.** When you
have paneled to within 4 feet of an irregular edge,
such as the edge of a fireplace, measure the
distance from the last panel installed to the farthest point on the fireplace edge. Mark this
distance on the panel to be cut, indicating the vertical line for the first, rough cut. For the horizontal cutting line, measure from the ceiling to
the mantel top—subtracting ¼ inch for the
clearance at the ceiling line (page 69)—and mark
this distance on the panel. Cut out the waste
rectangle defined by these measurements.

2 **Scribing the panel.** Set the newly cut edge of
the panel against the end of the mantel, keeping
the other edge plumb as it overlaps the last
panel installed. Place one leg of a pair of scribers
against the newly cut edge and rest the other
leg against the point on the fireplace edge farthest from it (the same point located in Step
1); tighten the scriber clamp to lock the legs in
this position. Starting at the top corner of the
mantel, and holding the legs of the scribers horizontal, transfer the outline of the fireplace
edge onto the panel. Cut the scribed line with a
saber saw or coping saw, then fit the contoured panel between the fireplace and the last
panel installed.

Usually the paneling continues across the top
of the fireplace and must be contoured to fit the
other side. First, measure 4 feet from the edge
of the last panel installed. From a plumb line
through this point, measure back to the most
distant point on the unpaneled edge of the fireplace and use the same procedure to mark
and cut a contoured panel for this side (inset).

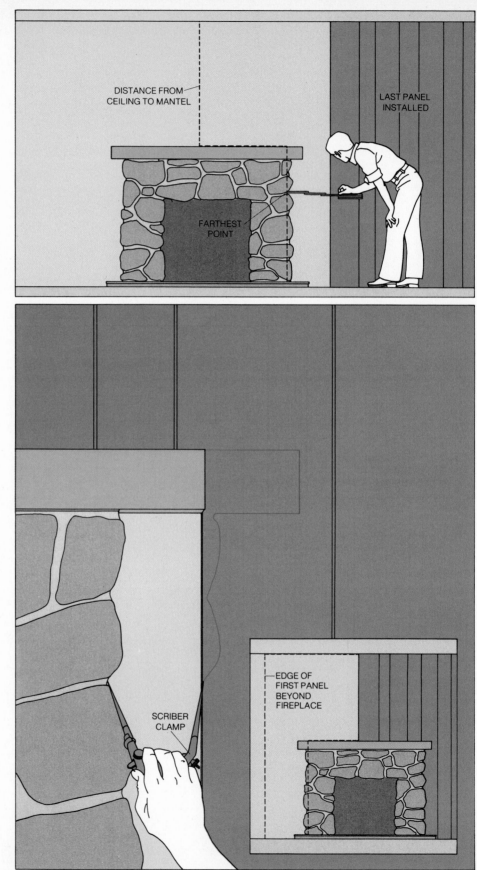

DISTANCE FROM
CEILING TO MANTEL

LAST PANEL
INSTALLED

FARTHEST
POINT

SCRIBER
CLAMP

EDGE OF
FIRST PANEL
BEYOND
FIREPLACE

Paneling Walls Higher than Eight Feet

Using horizontal molding. To cover a wall up to a high ceiling, install panels in two tiers—the first extending from the floor up 8 feet, the second butted against the first and continuing to the ceiling. Make sure the grooves of both tiers are aligned. Cover the horizontal joint between tiers with flat molding or a 1-inch-thick board finished to blend with the panels.

Using vertical molding. A second way to cover a wall up to a high ceiling is to install panels horizontally, stacking them one atop the other until they reach the ceiling. Align the grooves of abutting panels and cover the vertical joints with flat molding or 1-inch-thick boards that complement the panels. For smaller walls, you may prefer to break the horizontal line of the panels with vertical moldings placed at 4-foot intervals, as shown here.

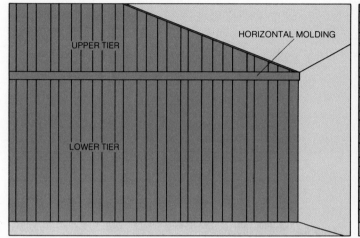

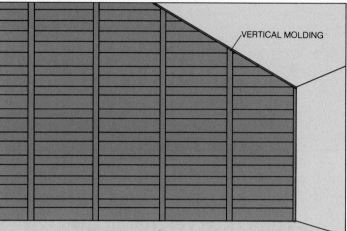

A Herringbone Pattern from Vertical Grooves

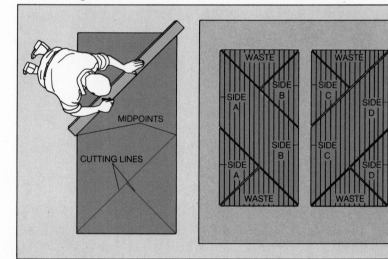

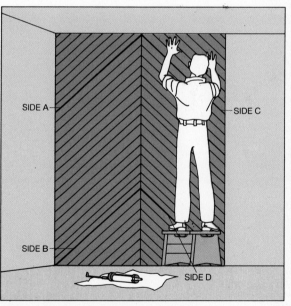

1 Marking the panels. On the back of a panel, mark the 4-foot midpoint of both sides. Draw a line from each midpoint to the diagonally opposite corner, using a long, straight board. Bisect the two diagonals with lines drawn from the other two corners. You will discard the top and bottom triangles as waste (*inset*). Label the sides of the other panel pieces as side A and side B.

Similarly mark a second panel, but reverse the direction of the diagonals and label the sides C and D. Saw both panels with a circular saw guided by a straight board (*page 70*).

2 Fitting the pieces. Join the panel sections that are lettered alike to create the herringbone pattern, butting together two A sides to form the top of a new rectangle and two B sides to form the bottom. Repeat this procedure for the C and D sides to form the adjoining rectangle, with the grooves running in the opposite direction. Install subsequent pairs of rectangles to form a continuous herringbone pattern, aligning the grooves from pair to pair.

An Expert Way with Moldings

In professional panel installations, every exposed edge except the inconspicuous vertical joint between panels is covered with a molding. Typically the moldings hide gaps at floor, ceiling and corners, speeding the installation by making precise measuring, scribing and cutting less essential. Moldings are sold—along with fillers used to conceal cracks—in colors and grain patterns to match the panels.

Panel moldings installed where walls meet floor and ceiling—the ones placed first—are usually much thinner and less expensive than ordinary floor and ceiling moldings, but are cut and installed in the same way. Along the floor, you join baseboard moldings at inside corners by coping, or trimming, one piece to fit snugly against the other. On outside corners at the floor, and at both inside and outside corners at ceilings, you join moldings by mitering the two pieces.

Instead of fancy crown moldings, small cove moldings are commonly used to finish panels at the ceiling line. Other small panel moldings—few of which measure even an inch wide—fit over the vertical joints between panels at inside and outside wall corners and cap the top edge of panels ending partway up a stairwell. In addition, cove and quarter-round moldings are sometimes used to cover the edges of panels where they meet brick walls or stairways.

To fasten the panel moldings, use the same colored paneling nails that are supplied by the manufacturer for fastening the panels. Space the nails at 16-inch intervals, starting at a stud or furring strip, and drive the nailheads below the surface with a nail set.

Fitting baseboard molding. To join floor moldings that meet at an inside corner, butt one piece of shaped molding against a wall and cut the second piece to fit the shape of the first in a two-step operation called coping. First, miter the end of the second piece of molding at an angle of 45°, cutting inward from back to front. Then run a pencil along the curved profile that is left on the face of the molding by the miter and, with a coping saw, cut straight through the molding along the marked curve, so that the end of the molding once again lies at right angles to the face. This will leave a shaped end that will fit against the face of the molding already on the wall (inset).

For an outside baseboard molding, simply miter both pieces of molding outward at an angle of 45° (46° if you want a nearly invisible joint). If the joint has a gap at the front or back, trim the molding until the two pieces meet to your satisfaction; use a small block plane to shave down front edges, a utility knife for back edges.

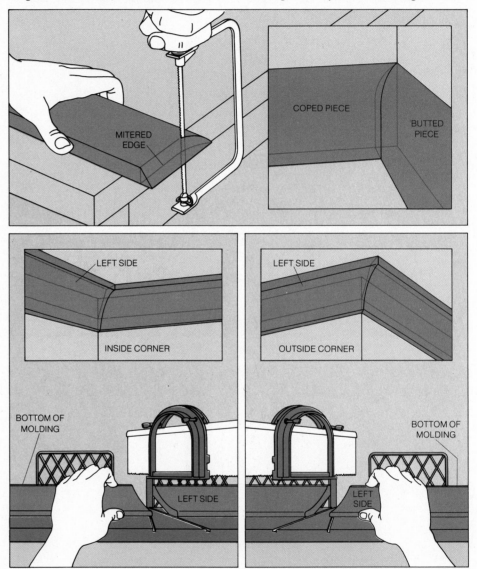

Ceiling moldings for an inside corner. Using a miter box, cut ceiling moldings at a 45° angle, placing the molding in the box upside down. Butt the two edges on the back of the molding, which are perpendicular to each other, against the bottom and back of the miter box. When you cut the left-hand molding, place it to the right of the saw blade, with the blade angled 45° to the right. When you cut the right-hand molding, place it to the left of the saw blade, with the blade angled 45° to the left.

Ceiling moldings for an outside corner. To cut ceiling molding to fit around an outside corner, place the molding in the miter box the same way as for an inside corner, upside down, with the left-hand molding to the right of the saw blade and the right-hand molding to the left of the saw blade. But for these cuts, the position of the saw blade has to be reversed—saw the left-hand molding with the saw blade angled 45° to the left, and saw the right-hand molding with the saw blade angled to the right.

Covering wall corners. At both inside and outside corners, butt the ends of the appropriately shaped molding, convex or concave (*inset*), between baseboard and ceiling molding. Fasten with nails every 12 inches. For an outside corner, drive the nails through alternate sides of the molding into the studs or furring strips backing the panel. For an inside corner, simply drive the nails into the center of the molding.

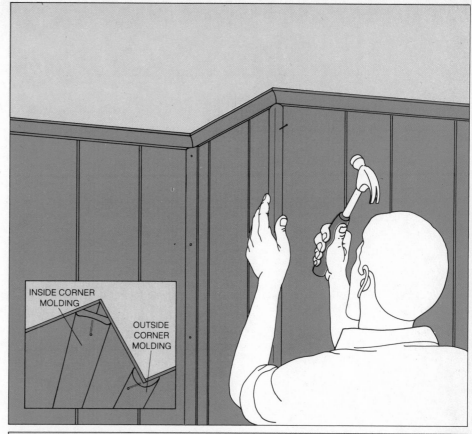

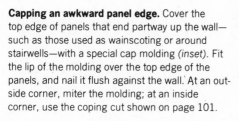

INSIDE CORNER MOLDING

OUTSIDE CORNER MOLDING

Capping an awkward panel edge. Cover the top edge of panels that end partway up the wall—such as those used as wainscoting or around stairwells—with a special cap molding (*inset*). Fit the lip of the molding over the top edge of the panels, and nail it flush against the wall. At an outside corner, miter the molding; at an inside corner, use the coping cut shown on page 101.

LIP

Solid-Wood Boards: An Elegant Way to Panel

A room paneled with boards is like a black dress with pearls—simple, tasteful and always in style. Whether you choose the classic rich hue of mahogany or the casual, rustic look of knotty pine, the room you adorn with solid wood will have a warmth and charm that can be achieved with few other wall coverings.

Many kinds of wood can be used for board paneling. Good hardwoods include birch, cherry, mahogany, maple, oak, pecan, rosewood, teak and walnut; popular softwoods are cedar, cypress, fir, hemlock, pine, redwood and spruce. Prices depend on the availability of the wood, which frequently varies with geographic location. Oak, for example, is more abundant, and therefore less expensive, on the East Coast of the United States. Some woods, such as mahogany or teak, are available only as imports and are always expensive.

The species of wood and the way you position the boards—vertically, horizontally or diagonally—have the greatest effect on the look of board paneling, but other factors are also important. Any board can be milled with a smooth or a rough-sawed surface. The grade of the wood can vary the effect, too—a clear grade provides an even, formal look; a knotty grade is more casual. Most boards are a nominal 1 inch thick (actually ¾ inch), but the width of boards ranges from 2 to 12 inches and varying widths are frequently intermixed on one wall.

Board edges may be square-cut for a contemporary look or they may be shaped with designs ranging from simple to elaborate, and milled to interlock or overlap. Those with interlocking tongue-and-groove joints are the easiest to work with, especially if the boards are installed in a diagonal pattern.

After you make the esthetic decisions, consider practical matters. Check availability and prices at several lumberyards in your area; ordering wood that is not stocked locally will add considerable shipping costs. Then calculate the square footage of the walls you will cover. Converting this figure into the number of board feet of lumber you need can be tricky, as it depends on the installation pattern, the average width of boards, and in some cases whether they are hardwood or softwood; ask your lumber dealer for help. Count on buying 10 to 20 per cent more than the minimum figure to cover inevitable waste.

Another consideration is board length. If you order in bulk, you will receive boards ranging in length from 8 to 14 feet. If you plan a diagonal installation that requires both short and long boards, a bulk order will serve your purpose best. But if you plan a vertical installation, it probably will be more economical to order boards all one length to minimize waste, although the price per board foot will be higher.

Once the planning and purchasing are done, you are ready for the installation. This task calls not so much for woodworking expertise as for patience and care, because wood boards have nonconforming personalities all their own. There is no way to avoid the slight cups, crooks, bows and twists that characterize wood. To keep all the boards exactly vertical, horizontal or diagonal, you must measure, cut and cajole each board into place individually, adjusting as you go.

Add to wood's normal idiosyncrasies the ravages wrought by years of exposure to the elements and you have barn boards, widely used for creating rustic-looking interiors. If you use barn boards, you can skip over decisions about color, grain, edge treatments and length. Barn boards come straight off the side of an old barn—their charm lies in their weathered appearance and in their irregularity, so you take what you can get.

Because barn boards are filled with nails, most mills refuse to machine-shape their edges to form joints. You put them up just as they are, trying out different arrangements to match the edges as well as possible. To make knotholes and gaps less conspicuous, cover the wall with black felt or black roofing paper before installing the boards.

Despite wood's many peculiarities, you can do an entire paneling job using a portable circular saw with a hollow-ground blade to cut the boards (a table or radial-arm saw is faster), a block plane to trim and smooth ends, and several measuring tools to keep you on course. You will need scribers, a level, a plumb bob, a steel square and a combination square. To guide the saw when you make miter or compound-miter cuts for a diagonal installation, you will also need a pair of plywood jigs with 45° angled edges, one sloping to the right, the other to the left (page 89, Step 2).

Plan to leave the boards in the room that is to be paneled for at least two days before you start installing them. Stack the boards in layers separated by 2-by-4s so they will become acclimated to the temperature and humidity of the room. This will reduce the wood's tendency to warp after installation.

While the boards acclimate, prepare the wall with furring. Horizontal strips, as shown on page 84, are adequate for vertical and diagonal patterns; furring for a herringbone installation is shown on page 92. Apply the furring strips using the techniques on pages 11-14, with one exception: Leave a ¾-inch space all around the opening for a door or window. Add jamb extensions (page 17, Step 2) only after all the boards are installed, when you are ready to put on the trim.

Choosing Patterns and Edges

A pattern for every purpose. Solid-wood paneling can be installed in one of several patterns. A vertical application is the most versatile—a traditional and formal look can be achieved with smooth, polished woods and elaborate trim, a contemporary look with rougher woods and a minimum of trim.

Dramatic diagonal and herringbone patterns are best in a modern setting. Boards on adjoining walls can be placed for a zigzag effect or to continue the same sloping line from one wall to the next. These patterns look best on walls with few doors or windows.

A horizontal application is the least common. In a high-ceilinged room, it can be exciting, but in a room of average height the pattern seems to lower the ceiling to an uncomfortable level.

Most professionals prefer to install solid boards without using base, ceiling or corner moldings, because these can detract from the bold, simple lines of the pattern. The door and window trim should be of the same wood as the paneling—strips cut with mitered corners to form a simple frame around the opening.

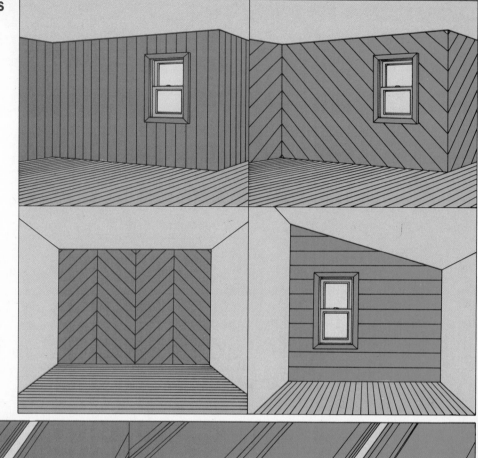

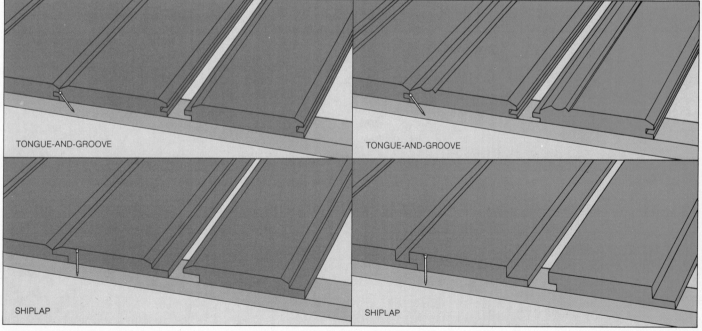

TONGUE-AND-GROOVE

TONGUE-AND-GROOVE

SHIPLAP

SHIPLAP

Milled edges for tight joints. Neat, gap-free joints that allow boards to expand and contract slightly with atmospheric changes are made possible by milled edges. Interlocking tongue-and-groove edges are the most common of these and are easy to install in any pattern. They can be milled so that the top edge of the joint is beveled, which creates a V-shaped seam between boards, or with rounded or even elaborately molded edges for a more decorative effect. Such boards are blind-nailed to furring strips through the base of the tongue; the nailheads are hidden by the next board.

Shiplap joints, where the edges of the boards do not interlock but do overlap each other, are easier to use in vertical or horizontal installation patterns than in diagonal ones. The boards typically come with their top edges beveled to form V-shaped seams, or with straight edges, which produce a slightly gapped joint. Shiplapped boards are generally nailed through the face of each board because nailing through the narrow edge tends to split the wood.

Straight edges for a modern look. Straight-edged boards and battens installed vertically or horizontally produce a casual, contemporary effect. Board-and-batten and reverse board-and-batten patterns are made of wide boards set about ½ inch apart with a narrower batten—generally a 1-by-2—nailed either over or under the gap. The contemporary-vertical pattern uses battens set on edge between the wider boards. Board-on-board paneling is similar to board-and-batten, except all the boards are the same width and the gap between boards in the first layer is about half the width of the boards. With any of these patterns, when face-nailing is necessary, forestall splitting by placing nails as far as possible from the board edges.

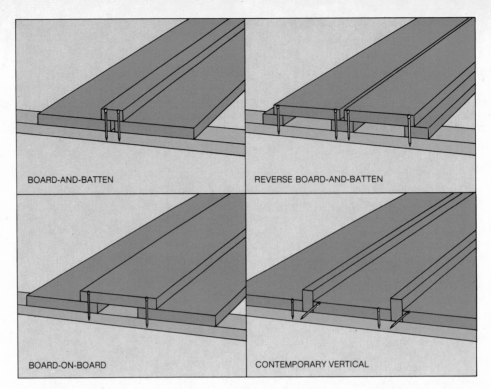

BOARD-AND-BATTEN

REVERSE BOARD-AND-BATTEN

BOARD-ON-BOARD

CONTEMPORARY VERTICAL

Installing the Classic Vertical Paneling

1 Planning the layout. To be sure the last board on a wall will not be a narrow strip, first calculate how many whole boards will fit on the wall by measuring the length of the wall in inches and dividing it by the width of a board (measured from its grooved edge to the base of the tongue). If the space for the last board is less than half a board width, determine how many inches are needed to widen it to half a board, then cut that amount from the grooved edge of the first board before you begin the installation.

2 **Starting off plumb.** Measure the starting corner from floor to ceiling and cut a board to that length, then set the board flat against the wall with its grooved edge abutting the adjoining wall. Check for plumb by holding a carpenter's level against the tongue edge of the board. If the grooved edge does not fit flush with the corner when the board is plumb—and if the space will not be covered by a board on the adjacent wall—scribe the board to match the corner, using the technique in Step 2, page 78, and trim the edge to the scribed line with a block plane.

If you install the first board at an outside corner, where the adjoining wall will not be paneled, trim ½ inch from the grooved edge of the board and place that cut edge plumb and flush with the corner. Plane as necessary for a precise fit.

3 **Nailing the first board.** Drive a sixpenny finishing nail at a 45° angle through the base of the tongue and into each horizontal furring strip, sinking the head with a nail set. If the board is wider than 6 inches, also face-nail it to every furring strip, a third of the way across the board from the grooved edge in the corner (*inset*). Sink the nailheads and cover with wood filler.

⅓ BOARD WIDTH

4 **Fitting individual boards.** To adjust each board to variations in ceiling height, cut a template—a board 3 inches shorter than the average ceiling height—and use it as a measuring device.

Place the template where the next board will go, rest it on the floor, and measure from the top of the template to the ceiling. Then lay the template on the board to be cut, bottom ends

flush, and transfer this measurement to it. Cut the board along this line, slide it into place on the wall, grooved edge over the tongue of the previous board, and nail it in place.

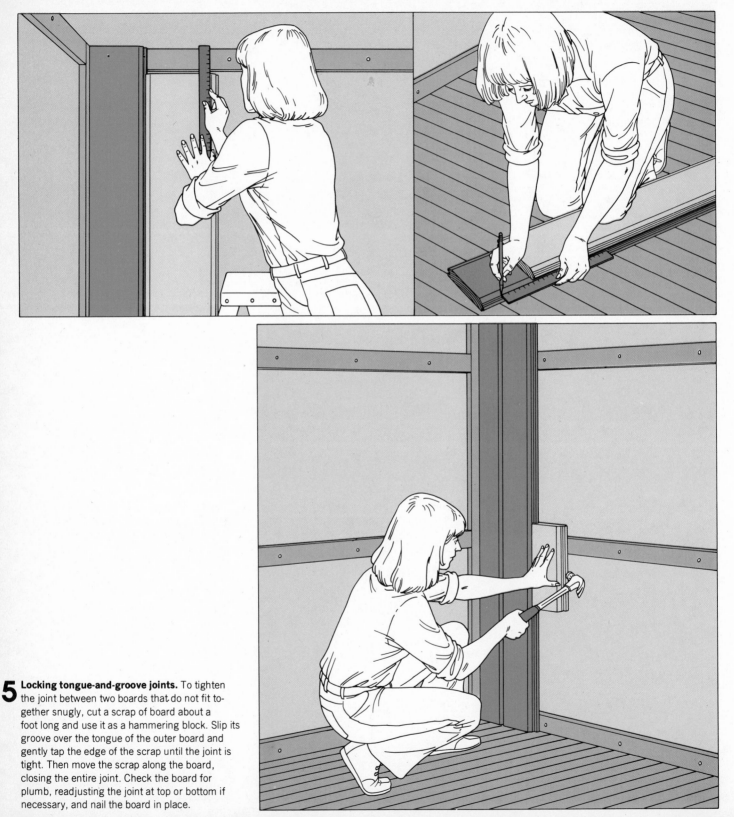

5 **Locking tongue-and-groove joints.** To tighten the joint between two boards that do not fit together snugly, cut a scrap of board about a foot long and use it as a hammering block. Slip its groove over the tongue of the outer board and gently tap the edge of the scrap until the joint is tight. Then move the scrap along the board, closing the entire joint. Check the board for plumb, readjusting the joint at top or bottom if necessary, and nail the board in place.

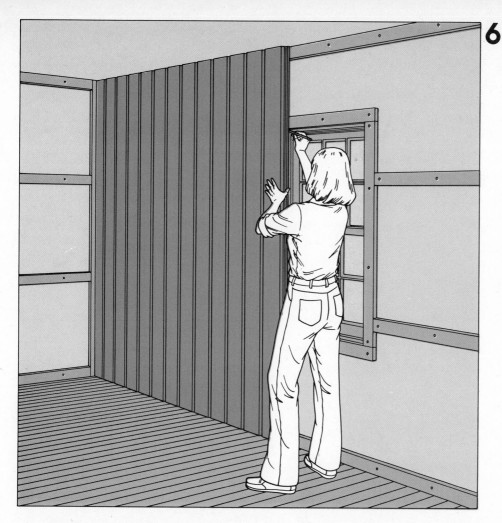

6 **Cutting to fit around an opening.** When you reach an opening, such as a window framed by furring strips *(page 11)*, lock the groove of a full-length board into position, with its tongue edge overlapping the opening. Reach behind the board and mark the back where it crosses the horizontal furring-strip edges closest to the opening. Mark the same furring strips where the tongue edge of the board crosses them. Then ease the board off the wall.

Measure the distance from the marks on the top and bottom furring strips to the edge of the vertical furring strip and transfer this measurement to the board at the top and bottom marks, drawing two lines that are perpendicular to the tongue edge. Connect the two lines with a third, parallel to the tongue edge. Drill ¼-inch pilot holes just inside the two corners formed by the three lines, then cut out the notch with a saber saw; the pilot holes will allow the blade to turn easily at the corners.

Measure and cut short boards to fit above and below the opening. Then cut a board to fit the other side of the opening in the same way.

Making Neat, Tight Corners

Mitering for an outside corner. Where paneling continues around a corner, lock the final board on the first wall into place, tongue edge extending beyond the corner, and mark the corner line on the back of the board. Remove the board and clamp it face down on two sawhorses with a straight-edged 1-by-2 strip on top to guide the saw. Set the blade of a circular saw at a 45° angle pointing toward the waste edge and make a beveled cut along the guideline. Lock and face-nail the board in place with the beveled edge extending beyond the corner *(inset)*.

To bevel the adjoining corner board, draw a guideline on the back of the board, marking the desired width of the board as determined in Step 1; measure this distance from the tongue edge. Then clamp the board face down and cut along the line, with the saw blade angled toward the grooved edge of the board. Before setting the board in place, spread wood glue on both beveled edges; then tape them together until the glue dries. Trim the corner with a block plane.

Snugging boards at an inside corner. After locking the next-to-last board in place, pull its tongue edge slightly away from the wall, slip on the grooved edge of the final board and push both boards against the wall at once. Face-nail the boards as in Step 3, page 85. To ensure a tight fit—especially important in a corner where no adjoining paneling will cover the edge of the final board—cut the final board exactly to size, scribing the cut edge, if necessary, to conform to the corner. Then use a block plane to bevel the corner edge about 5° toward the back face of the board (inset).

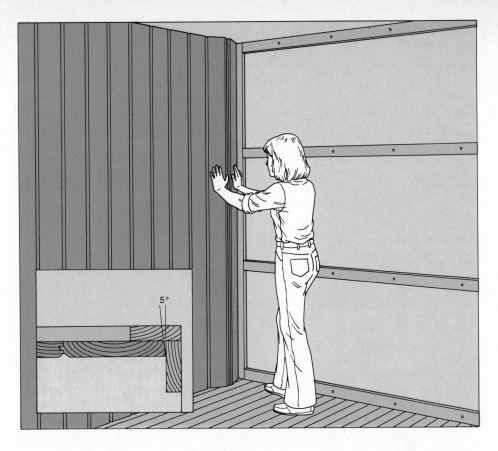

Diagonals for Dramatic Flair

1 Laying out a 45° starting line. Snap a plumb chalk line from ceiling to floor about 6 inches from the corner of the wall and draw a horizontal line across it about 2 feet from the floor. Mark each of the lines 3 feet from their intersection and connect these marks with a diagonal line. Extend the diagonal line across the wall as far as it will go.

Construct this diagonal starting line in the direction you want the boards to run. Keep the starting line as low on the wall as possible because it is easier to work upward, pushing each board down over the tongue edge of the one that preceded it. Make the diagonal about 6 feet long—long enough to ensure that the angle of the first board is accurate, since it sets the angle for the entire wall. Also, be sure the starting line does not lap over a door or window.

If the projected paneling reverses direction on an adjoining wall, forming an inverted V pattern, construct a second starting line, using the first for reference. Measure from the corner to the bottom of the first starting line; then mark off this distance along the bottom of the adjoining wall. Snap a diagonal line between this mark and the top of the first starting line (inset).

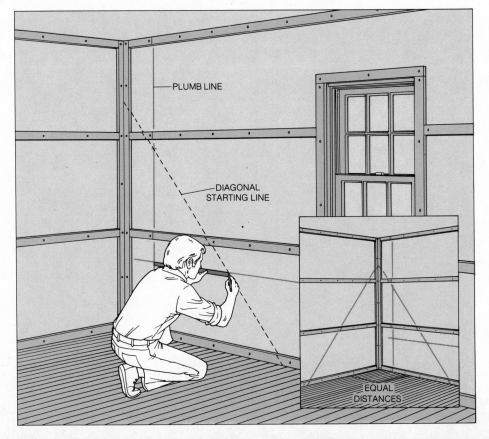

PLUMB LINE

DIAGONAL STARTING LINE

EQUAL DISTANCES

2 **Cutting boards to fit.** Using a circular saw and a diagonal jig (*inset*), cut a 45° miter at each end of the board, making sure that the direction of each miter matches the surface that the board will butt against—the floor, wall, ceiling, door or window. To cut the first board, measure the length of the starting line and transfer the measurement to the grooved edge of the board, then start the cuts at that edge. To cut consecutive boards, measure the length of the tongue edge on the previous board.

When more than one board length is needed for a long diagonal, cut the two board ends square and butt them together; glue the joint. Stagger these butted joints as you go up the wall so that they will not line up together.

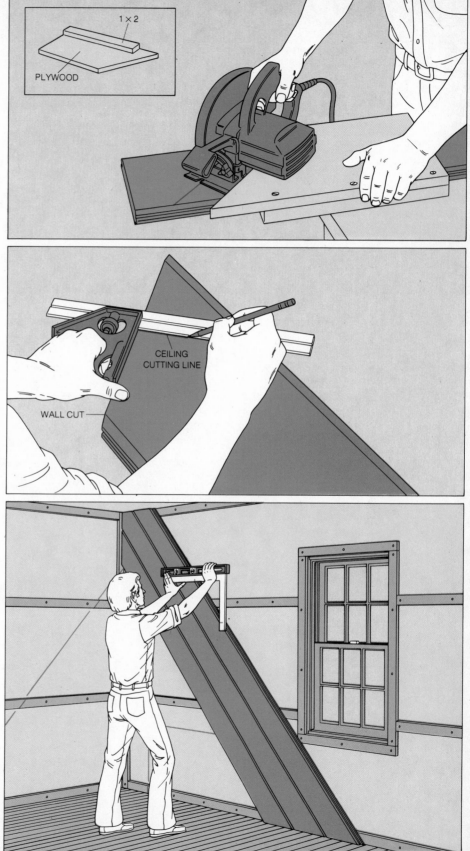

3 **Measuring double-angle cuts.** When the end of a board hits two surfaces perpendicular to each other—such as the ceiling and a corner of the wall—first miter the end to fit flush with one of the two surfaces (in this example, the wall). Then measure how much of the wall corner remains to be covered by paneling, and mark off this distance on the mitered end, measuring from the grooved edge. Use a combination square to draw a perpendicular line from the mark to the tongue edge of the board, and make the second cut—here, the ceiling cut—along that line.

4 **Maintaining a 45° angle.** Check the angle of each board after you position it, by holding a steel square against it, lining up the two 12-inch marks on the square with the tongue edge of the board. Place a carpenter's level on the horizontal arm of the square, and adjust the board until the arm is level; then nail the board in place.

5 **Flanking an opening with a diagonal.** Lock a board in places it overlaps the corner of the window or door opening, check its angle (*page 89, Step 4*), then reach behind the board to mark where the back of the tongue edge crosses the furring strips at each side of the opening. Remove the board, lay it face down, and use a steel square to draw a right angle between the two marks (*inset*). Cut out the angle with a saber saw, then nail the board in place.

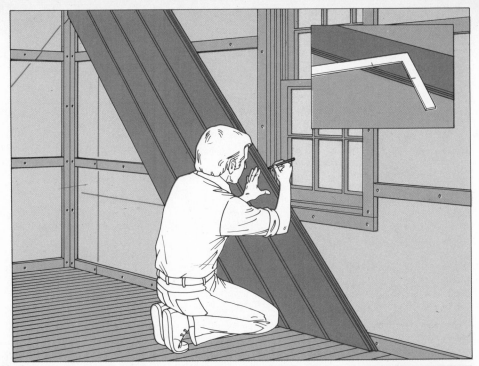

COMPOUND MITER

WASTE END

6 **Beveling boards at an outside corner.** To install the first board that meets the corner of the wall, miter both ends and lock the board in place in the usual fashion. At the bottom end of the board, mark the part that extends beyond the corner by drawing a line across the back of the board. Then remove the board and clamp it, face down, across two sawhorses. Set the blade of a circular saw at a 45° angle pointing toward the waste end of the board. Using a diagonal jig to guide the saw, cut along the marked line; this will create a compound miter—an edge that is both

mitered and beveled. Lock the board in place, with the compound miter extending beyond the corner (*inset*), and nail it.

On subsequent boards, miter the top but leave the bottom end temporarily unmitered. Lock the board in place, mark the part that extends beyond the corner by drawing a pencil line across the back, then cut a compound miter along this line. At the top of the wall, where the last board is simply a small triangle, use wood glue as well as nails to help anchor the board to the furring.

7 **Trimming lower boards for easier fit.** Working down from the starting board, miter the boards to fit, but here use the grooved edge of the previous board as a measure. On the shorter boards near the bottom corner, trim several inches from each end of the tongue with a utility knife; this makes it easier to get the tongue into the groove of the board above.

Check the angle and nail the board in place. Anchor the triangular last board at the foot of the wall with wood glue as well as nails.

Carrying the Pattern around a Corner

Turning an inside corner. Cut the first board for the second wall as in Step 2, page 89, using the previously drawn starting line as a measure. Butt the board firmly against the corresponding board on the other wall, forming an inverted V at the corner. Then cut and install succeeding boards, always taking care to match each board to its mate on the adjoining wall.

Joining boards at an outside corner. Where a diagonal pattern shifts direction at an outside corner, forming a V, choose a reference board on the first wall. Note where its lower edge meets the ceiling, locate a corresponding point on the adjoining ceiling and draw a diagonal starting line from that point down to where the lower edge of the reference board meets the corner (*inset*).

Then miter one end of the first board, butt it against the ceiling, and line up the other end with its mate on the adjoining wall. Have a helper hold the board at the starting line but slightly away from the wall, to allow for the protruding miter of its mate, while you mark a cutting line for the compound miter on the back of the board. Transfer the cutting line to the front of the board.

Clamp the board, face up, across two sawhorses, set the circular saw at a 45° angle pointing away from the waste end and, using a diagonal jig to guide the saw, cut slightly outside the marked line to allow for trimming the final joint. Spread wood glue on the mitered end and when the board is nailed in place, tape the mitered ends together until the glue dries.

Mark, cut and attach all the remaining boards in the same way. When all the boards are in place, use a block plane to smooth the corner.

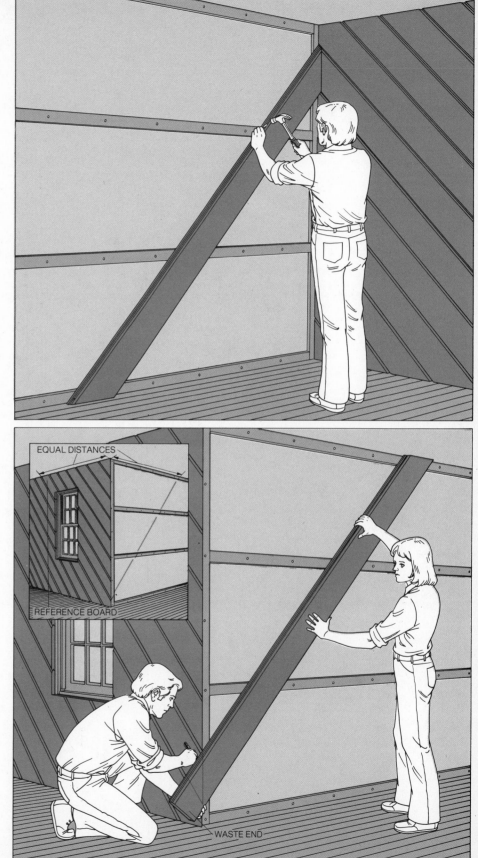

EQUAL DISTANCES

REFERENCE BOARD

WASTE END

A Herringbone with Boards

1 **Installing the furring strips.** With baseboard and ceiling molding removed, divide the wall vertically into equal parts, marking each division with a plumb chalk line. Frame the perimeter of the wall with 1-by-4 furring strips, then center and nail a furring strip over each chalk line. Snap a second chalk line down the center of each strip.

Tack a temporary 1-by-2 batten to the first furring strip, as a guide for the mitered ends of the first group of boards. Be sure to select a batten with perfectly straight edges and set the batten flush with the chalk line.

2 **Attaching the first board.** Starting at a lower corner of the first wall section, cut and install the first board—a right triangle with two equal sides. Glue and nail the board in place, butting the two equal sides against the floor and the batten. To mark the cutting lines for the triangle, place a steel square on the board as shown (*inset*), its corner against the grooved edge.

Measure, cut and install diagonal boards to complete the first wall section, using the technique described in Steps 2 through 6, pages 89-91. Align one end of each board with the edge of the wall, the other end with the batten.

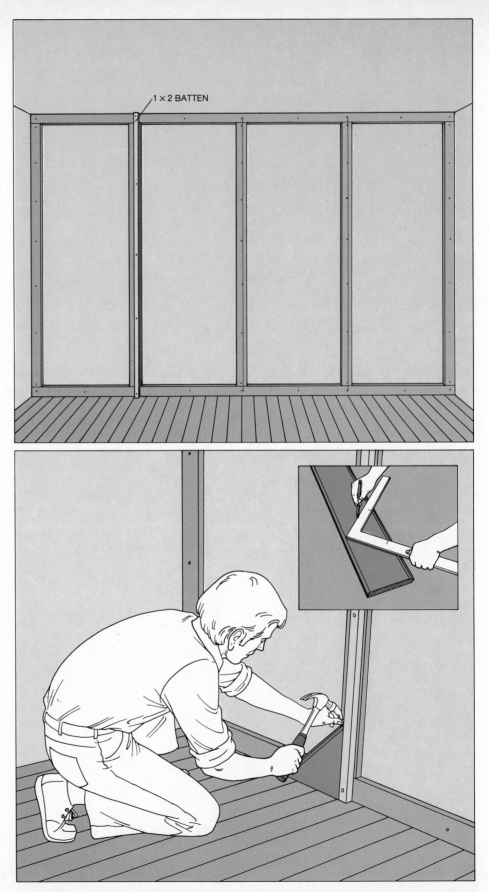

1 × 2 BATTEN

3 **Completing the herringbone.** Remove the batten from the first furring strip and tack it flush with the chalk line on the second furring strip. Install the next section of diagonal boards, beginning with a triangle as before but working from the opposite corner so the boards run in the opposite direction. Make sure each board butts squarely against its corresponding board in the first section, to form a V. Continue across the wall, installing one section at a time.

A Choice of Finishes for Fine Wood

There are several ways to finish a wall of solid-wood paneling, depending on the appearance and the amount of protection you want. A few woods, such as cedar and redwood, are prized for their rugged naturalness and they age so beautifully that they are generally left unfinished. Most woods, however, require some sort of finishing.

Professionals usually stain the wood and then cover it with a clear, protective coating. If you want a stain finish, it is best to apply it after the boards are in place. You can purchase boards already stained, but they are considerably more expensive than the unstained kind. Also, you run the risk of marring the finish during installation.

The stains easiest to get and to use are the oil-based. Water-based and alcohol-based stains—the two other types—both have drawbacks. Water-based stains tend to raise the grain of the wood, necessitating extra sanding. Alcohol-based stains are dangerous and difficult to use—the stain must be dissolved in hot alcohol and applied very quickly to prevent streaking.

In choosing a stain, consider the natural color of the wood as well as the colors in the furnishings. Also remember that all woods darken with age.

Pine, as it darkens, becomes more yellow; oak turns a russet brown. The wood will darken whether it is stained or not—the main function of the stain is to enhance the wood's natural color and emphasize its grain.

Light-brown tones are generally best for light woods like pine, birch and oak, although birch is sometimes stained to resemble cherry or mahogany. Dark woods like walnut and mahogany may be stained deeper tones but are often left unstained.

Plan to stain an entire wall at once. The job requires two people—one to apply the stain with a brush, sponge or specially textured glove; the other to follow behind and wipe off the stain with a rag after the prescribed number of minutes. When the stain is dry, apply a clear finish to protect the wood from dirt and scratches. For that matter, unstained wood should be similarly protected. Three types of protective coatings can be used—oil-based sealers, shellacs or varnishes.

Oil-based sealers are easy to apply and leave a muted, mat finish that can be polished to a soft luster with a coating of paste furniture wax. This finish is easy to touch up and provides moderate protection. If you require tough-

er protection, use shellac or varnish.

Although varnish dries harder than shellac and is virtually impermeable, most experts prefer shellac for wall paneling. It brushes on easily and dries in about 10 minutes, while varnish is more difficult to apply and takes 24 hours to dry—during which time dust may settle on the sticky surface and mar the finish. Varnishes are also finicky: They will not adhere over some stains. Ask your paint dealer for compatible stain and varnish. Since varnishes have a tendency to darken the wood more than shellac, you may want to choose a slightly lighter shade of stain.

If, for durability, you do choose varnish, use a linseed-and-alkyd type. Polyurethane varnish is tougher and is recommended for furniture that takes a real beating. But few walls need such protection and polyurethane varnish produces noxious fumes.

If you use shellac, ask for 4-pound cut—a mixture of 4 pounds of shellac diluted in 1 gallon of alcohol. Dilute it further by combining 1 part of the mixture with 2 parts alcohol to produce a thin liquid that spreads evenly. Apply four coats. If you want to cut the shine, rub the final coat with steel wool and add a coat of paste wax.

The Cabinetmaker's Art Displayed on a Wall

Few wood wall coverings can match the grace and joinery of Georgian paneling—the raised paneling perfected by 18th Century artisans. Made of wood rectangles whose beveled edges are clinched between vertical stiles and horizontal rails, this traditional wall covering is most often associated with posh clubs and law offices, but it can bring a classical elegance to any room.

With the proper tools, you can make authentic raised paneling of solid wood. Or, to save time and money, you can create a facsimile by adding stiles, rails, and other embellishments to flat plywood panels. Softwoods were traditionally used for raised paneling; some, like clear white pine, can be stained and varnished for rich color and grain. Or you can finish the paneling with paint, as was common in colonial times.

There are choices, too, in the treatment of details. With solid-wood paneling, you can leave the edges of stiles and rails square or shape them with a router. With frame-on-plywood paneling, you can add a rectangle of molding several inches within the frame of stiles and rails, or add a raised panel of ⅛-inch hardboard with beveled edges. These bevels are naturally much narrower than those on solid-wood panels, and the entire assembly must be painted, rather than stained.

With either type of paneling, the planning stage is crucial. Make a scale drawing of the existing wall, showing door and window openings, electric switches and outlets, and any other protruding fixtures. Then superimpose a sketch of the paneling on this drawing. A common pattern (below) uses four levels of rails: one near the floor, a second about 32 inches above the floor, a third just above the tops of doors and windows, and a fourth just below the ceiling.

The width of individual panels should not exceed 24 inches, except at doors and windows, where the frame should be wide enough to span the opening. Plan the frame layout so that each hole for an electric switch or outlet will fall on a flat surface, rather than on a joint or a section of molding; you may have to move electrical elements or have a licensed electrician do so. For frame-on-plywood paneling, position stiles to cover the joints between plywood panels.

The width of stiles, rails and moldings depends on the proportions of the wall, but it should fall within a general range—stiles, 4 to 6 inches; rails, 2½ to 3½ inches; base moldings, 3½ to 5 inches; crown moldings, 3 inches; door and window casings, 3 inches. Refine your sketch to include these dimensions, then transfer your pattern directly to the wall; if the proportions seem correct and the pieces are properly positioned, you are ready to begin building.

For frame-on-plywood paneling, which is assembled directly on the wall, use furniture-grade ¼-inch plywood, and paint or stain it before installing it. Nail it to furring strips attached to the wall in the pattern used for regular plywood, but add horizontal furring strips at rail heights. Solid-wood paneling is fastened to the wall in completed sections.

To make frame-on-plywood paneling, you need no special tools, but for the special cuts and joints of raised paneling, you will need a doweling jig, router and table saw. For best results, use grooved dowels for secure glue bonding, and use carbide-tipped router bits that have ball-bearing guides, called pilots.

For work with the table saw, you will need a dado head, a combination of blades that makes a wider cut than one blade alone. You will also need special wooden guides on the saw table: one bolted to the rip fence, the other parallel to the rip fence on the opposite side of the blade. To speed production, finish each step for all the pieces before proceeding to the next step.

The Structure of a Wall of Raised Panels

Dissecting the parts. Stiles (vertical) and rails (horizontal), made of ¾-inch boards, secure the panels. The interlocked stiles and rails have glued dowel joints and their edges are dadoed (grooved) to hold the beveled panel edges.

The bottom rail (inset, bottom) rests on blocking made of inexpensive ¾-inch lumber slightly narrower than the base molding that covers it, and the whole structure is nailed to the furring strips behind the edges of every rail, and behind the top and bottom blocking. One third of the way up the wall, chair-rail molding covers a joint between frame sections. Crown molding trims the wall near the ceiling (inset, top), and casings border the doors and windows. At floor level on both sides of the door are rectangular plinth blocks, which separate the curves of door casing from those of base molding.

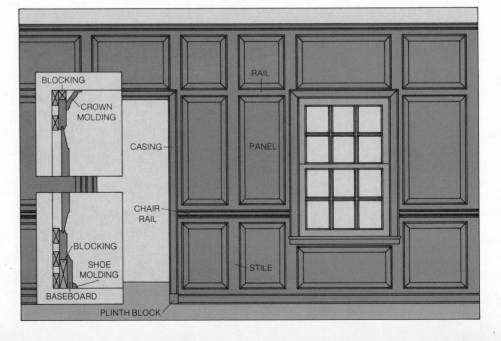

A Facsimile with Plywood

1 **Laying out the frame.** With a pencil and a long straight-edged board, mark positions for the edges of stiles and rails on the plywood-paneled wall, making sure that all joints between panels will be covered by stiles and that no stile or rail edge will cross an electric outlet or switch. Mark the position of the bottom edge of the bottom rail; it should be 1 inch lower than the height of the planned base molding. Finally, cut all of the stiles, making them ½ inch shorter than the overall wall height for ease in installation.

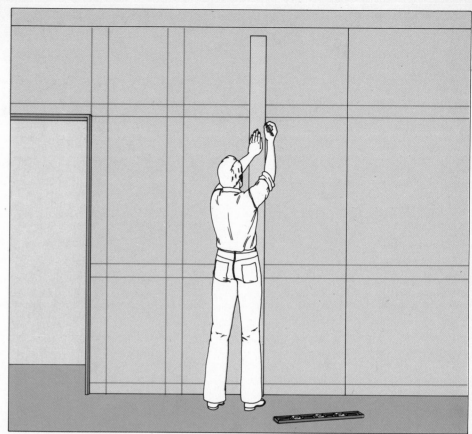

2 **Attaching the stiles and rails.** Line up a stile with one set of stile-edge marks, checking it with a level for plumb. Nail the stile in place with eight-penny finishing nails long enough to reach through stile and paneling to the horizontal furring strips; use two nails at each strip. Nail the other stiles in place, then measure and cut rails for a snug fit between stiles, using a miter box to ensure perfectly square rail ends. Line up the rails with the pencil marks and tap them into position with a mallet, placing a wood block between mallet and rail. Nail the rails in place.

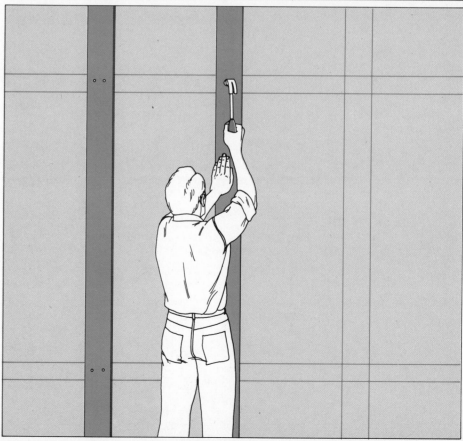

3 **Adding mitered molding.** Finish the edges of stiles and rails with mitered quarter-round or patterned molding (*page 35*), installed so the mitered cuts slant inward and the overall length of the molding equals the distance along a stile or rail. Nail the molding in place with 1-inch brads, starting with a stile and working clockwise around to the remaining three sides of the rectangle. Repeat for each frame, then fill any cracks at miter joints with wood putty.

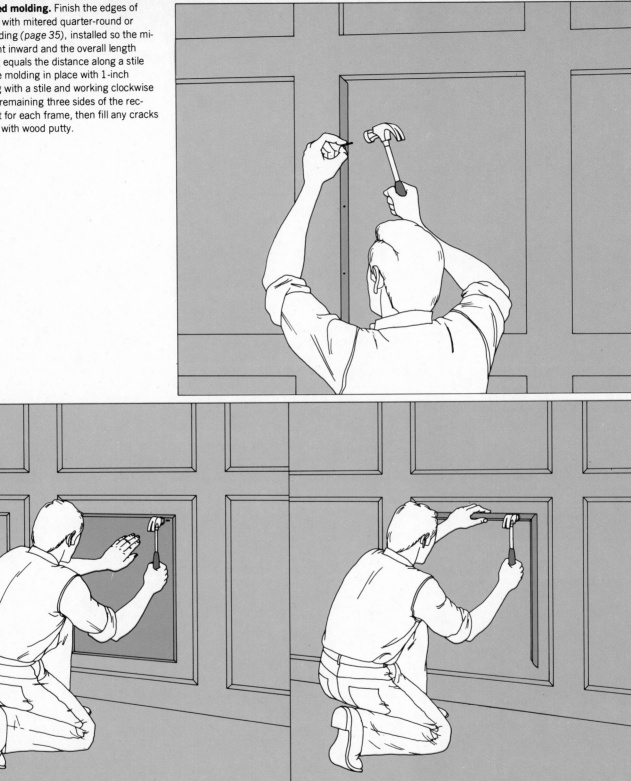

4 **Adding embellishments.** For a raised-panel effect in the rectangle (*above, left*), cut a piece of ⅛-inch hardboard 2 inches shorter and narrower than the inside measure of the rectangle. Bevel its edges with a table saw, then center it

and attach it with glue and ¾-inch brads. Repeat for the other rectangles.

Alternatively, add a molding rectangle of the same dimensions and location as the raised panel

described above (*above, right*). Outline its position in pencil, then use the technique described in Step 3 to nail mitered molding along the outline. Repeat for the other rectangles. Countersink all nails and fill holes with wood putty.

Building a Frame for Solid-Wood Panels

1 Laying out a frame. Nail horizontal furring strips to the wall along the floor and the ceiling, at each rail level and at the midpoint between any rails more than 2 feet apart (*pages 13-14*). Nail blocking over the strip at floor level (*page 94*) and mark the exact positions of stile edges on all the strips. Also, mark for the joint between top and bottom sections of the panels. The strips must be wider than the rails or doubled so that each rail edge is backed by furring.

Use the stile-edge marks to calculate the exact stile, rail and panel dimensions. Stiles for the bottom section of panels reach from the top of the blocking to the joint line; stiles for the top section reach from the joint line to 2 inches below the ceiling. Measure the distance between stile edges to determine rail lengths. If you plan to shape the edges of stiles and rails, allow for this decorative edge in calculating the length of the rail, which must meet the stile at the break line (*inset*) where the shaped edge begins.

Cut stiles and rails, lay them face down on the floor in the relative positions they will occupy on the wall, and mark rail and stile with matching numbers at each joint, to speed later assembly.

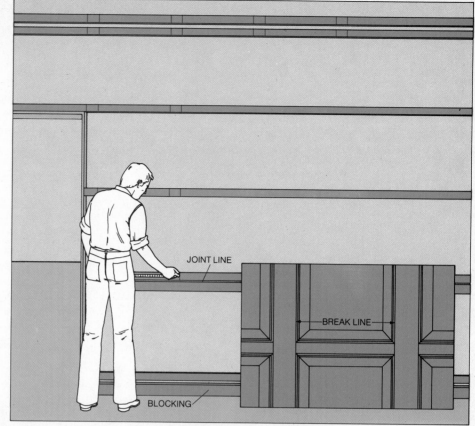

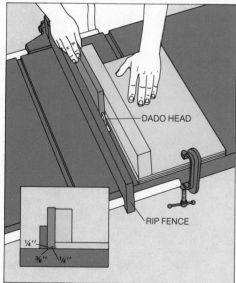

2 Cutting grooves in rails and stiles. Assemble a ¼-inch dado head on the table saw and lock the rip fence ⅜ inch from the near edge of the dado head. Clamp an auxiliary fence—a 2-by-4 nailed to a piece of plywood—to the saw table on the other side of the blade, separated from the rip fence by the thickness of the lumber used for stiles and rails. Set the dado head to cut ¼ inch above the table. With the power on, feed rails and stiles—one edge down and the outside face against the rip fence—over the dado head.

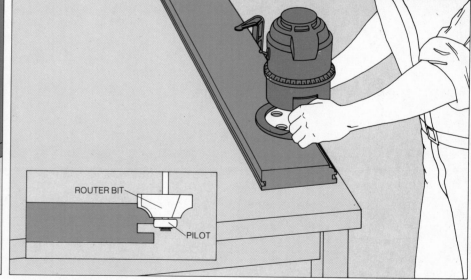

3 Shaping stile and rail edges. Clamp a stile, face up, on a worktable and put the desired edge-forming bit in a router. Rest the router base on the stile face with the bit an inch or so in from one end of the stile; turn on the router and push it toward the stile until the pilot comes into contact with the edge of the wood (*inset*). Slowly move the router to the near end of the stile until the bit clears the corner, then move the router in the opposite direction, shaping the entire edge of the stile.

If the clamp blocks the router, switch off the motor, reposition the clamp, and then restart the shaping cut an inch away from the stopping point, bringing the pilot against the still-uncut edge of the stile.

Shape the opposite edge of the stile in the same way, then repeat the shaping process on all the remaining stiles and rails except along those edges that are going to be covered by chair-rail molding, door casing or base molding.

4 **Preparing a shaped stile for joints.** On the back of a stile that has a shaped edge, mark the points where the rail edges intersect the stile. Then use a combination square (*below, left*) to mark the converging lines of a 45° angle from these points. Use a tenon saw or other fine-tooth saw (*below, right*) to cut along the lines, down to the break line of the shaped edge. Keep the cutting edge of the saw horizontal. Repeat wherever a rail intersects a stile.

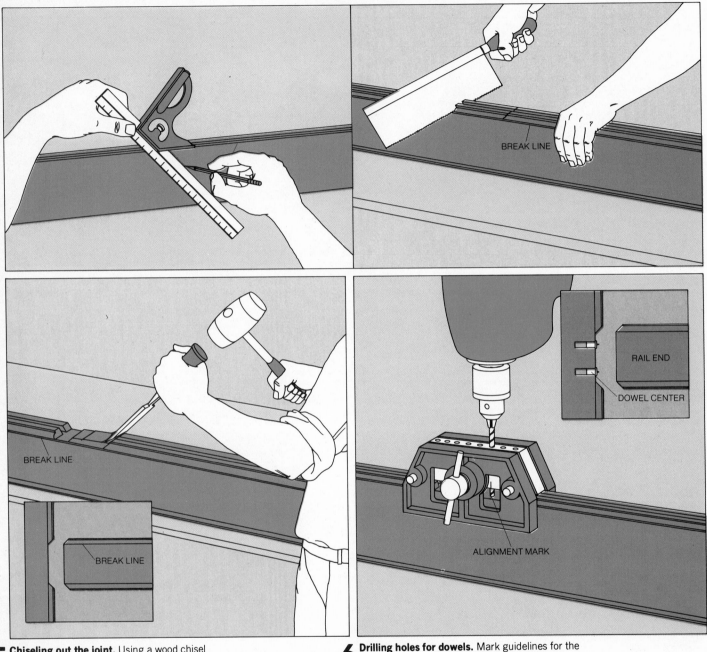

BREAK LINE

BREAK LINE

BREAK LINE

RAIL END

DOWEL CENTER

ALIGNMENT MARK

5 **Chiseling out the joint.** Using a wood chisel with the beveled edge facing down, remove the wood between saw cuts. Chisel off chips about ¾ inch long and 1/16 inch thick until you have a flat surface at the level of the break line.

Use a miter box to cut a 45° angle across each corner of the matching rail. Position the rail for the cut by aligning the saw blade over the point where the break line intersects the rail end (*inset*). Repeat for all other rails.

6 **Drilling holes for dowels.** Mark guidelines for the doweling jig by drawing lines across both ends of the cutout section of a stile, ½ inch in from the bottom of the bevel. Center the jig over each line and drill a 5/16-inch hole, 1⅛ inches deep. Slide a 5/16-inch metal dowel center into each of the holes (*inset*); align the matching rail and tap its free end to force the points of the dowel centers into the wood. Then remove the rail, align the jig over the dowel-center marks, and drill holes in the rail to match those in the stile.

Cutting and Assembling the Raised Panels

1 **Joining boards edge-to-edge.** Select several ¾-inch-thick boards long enough to make one or two raised panel sections and with a combined width slightly greater than the planned width of one panel. Lay the boards edge-to-edge across pipe clamps positioned near the board ends and at 20-foot intervals. Place additional clamps across the top of the boards parallel to and mid-way between those on the bottom; then tighten all the clamps, increasing the pressure evenly until the seams between boards are nearly invisible hairlines.

If there are still gaps between the boards, remove the clamps and carefully recut the board edges on a table saw that has been fitted with a sharp carbide-tipped blade. Test the boards again in the clamps.

When no gaps show between board edges, loosen the clamps, spread a film of carpenter's glue on each board edge and reclamp the boards. After the glue is dry, remove the clamps, cut the panels to size, and sand the faces.

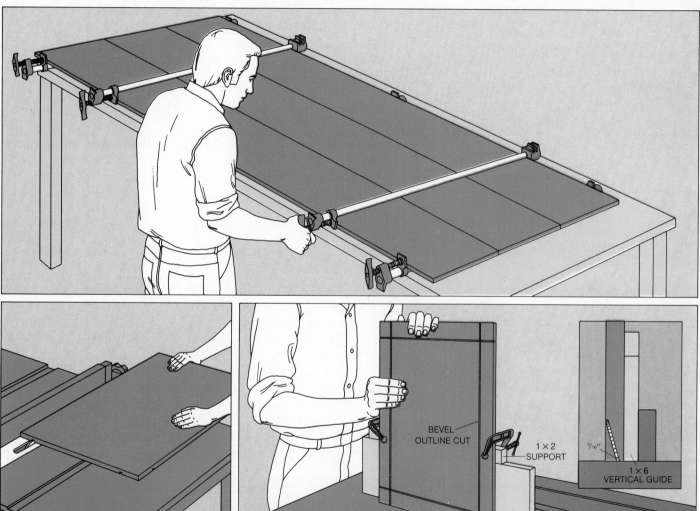

BEVEL OUTLINE CUT

1 × 2 SUPPORT

3/16″

1 × 6 VERTICAL GUIDE

2 **Outlining the bevel.** Set the cutting height of a table-saw blade at ¹/₁₆ inch and position the rip fence 2 inches from the blade. Hold a panel face down, one edge against the rip fence, and make a shallow cut down the length of the panel face, ¹/₁₆ inch deep. Repeat the same cut 2 inches in from the other three edges of the panel. Outline the bevels for all the panels in this way, and make similar cuts on several pieces of scrap the same thickness as the panels, to use in setting the saw blade for the bevel cut.

3 **Cutting the bevel.** To set up the saw, tilt the blade away from the rip fence at a 15° angle, and fasten a 1-by-6 board to the rip fence as a vertical guide, anchoring the guide to the fence with countersunk flat-head stove bolts. Then position the guide so that its face is ³/₁₆ inch away from the saw blade at table level, and adjust the cutting height of the blade so that the highest part of the blade reaches exactly to the bevel outline you have drawn on one of the pieces of scrap lumber (*inset*).

Slide a panel into the space between the blade and the vertical guide, with the back of the panel against the guide and the end grain down. To steady the panel, rest a length of 1-by-2 on top of the guide and clamp the panel and the 1-by-2 together. Turn on the saw and, keeping your hands well above the table, push the panel over the blade. Repeat this procedure on the opposite end of the panel, and then on the two sides, repositioning and reclamping the 1-by-2 support before each cut.

Assembling the Pieces and Erecting the Wall

1 Joining the parts. Place the panels, rails and stiles of the lower paneling section face down on the floor, with the adjoining edges facing each other and the bottom edge toward the wall. Using a wooden mallet, first tap 2-inch-long dowels into all of the rail holes; then tap panels into the rail grooves; finally, tap stiles onto the dowels protruding from the rails.

If the joints fit tightly, as they should, disassemble the parts, spread a thin film of glue inside the dowel holes and on all of the facing edges of the joints—but not in the grooves. Reassemble the parts, using pipe clamps stretched from stile to stile to close the joints. Drive ½-inch brads through the backs of rails and stiles into both ends of all dowels. Then remove the clamps and assemble the remaining sections in the same way.

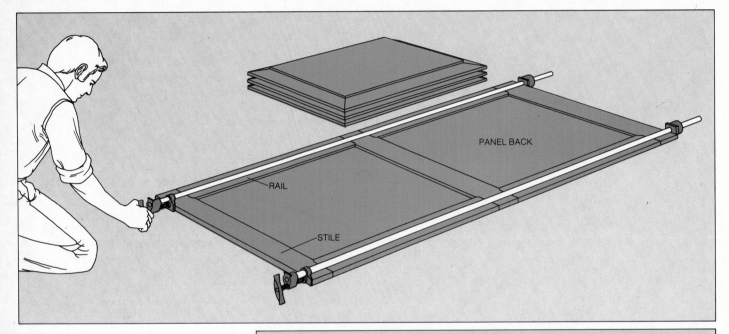

PANEL BACK

RAIL

STILE

2 Raising the paneling. With helpers providing support at each stile, tilt the lower paneling section against the wall, then lift it and set the bottom rail on the blocking. Slide a carpenter's level along the top of the paneling while a helper wedges thin wooden shims between the blocking and the bottom rail to level the section. Fasten the stiles to the wall at each furring strip with pairs of eightpenny finishing nails.

Raise the upper paneling section into position on top of the lower one, aligning the stiles exactly, and nail the upper stiles to the furring strips. Nail blocking between the top rail and the ceiling. When all sections are in place, cover the joint between the upper and lower sections with chair rail, and add ceiling, corner and base moldings (*pages 80-81*). Frame the door and window openings with casings that match the wood of the stiles and rails. Use a nail set to countersink all nails, and fill the holes with wood putty.

BLOCKING

Wainscoting: Hip-High Panels with Top Trim

Not all wall paneling rises from floor to ceiling—some stops short and is called wainscoting, a term that originally meant "the wooden sides of a wagon." Wainscot paneling can vary in height from 30 to 36 inches, but it generally looks best when it is no more than one third the height of the wall.

Wainscoting can be made of solid wood or plywood, and can be flat, or patterned with raised panels constructed the same way as the full-height variety described on the preceding pages. In construction wainscoting differs from floor-to-ceiling paneling only in the molding that covers the upper edge. One-piece cap molding serves as the top trim for thin wainscoting, but thicker panels, or ones nailed to furring strips, require wider and sometimes more elaborate assemblies of two or three different pieces of molding.

Ordinarily, top trim is mitered or square-cut, but in some situations you may want to use more sophisticated techniques. At inside corners that are not perfect right angles—or if you prefer fancier joinery—you can forgo simple mitering and use the more traditional coping cut (bottom, left). Similarly, if you plan to set the top molding at the same height as the window stool (the inside extension of the window sill), you will need to scribe and then cut the top molding in much the same fashion as that outlined in Step 2, page 78.

Making a Wainscot of Plywood or Solid Wood

Wainscot and top trim. When ¼-inch plywood paneling is used for wainscoting and is fastened directly to the wall, the easiest trim to apply is cap molding, already factory-cut to lap over the panel edge (*below, left*). But if paneling protrudes farther than the depth of the cap molding—which is generally ¼ inch—you can use window-stool stock, rip-cut to the desired width and finished with base-cap molding above and cove molding beneath (*below, right*). At the floor, regular baseboard and shoe molding serve as trim for both types of wainscoting.

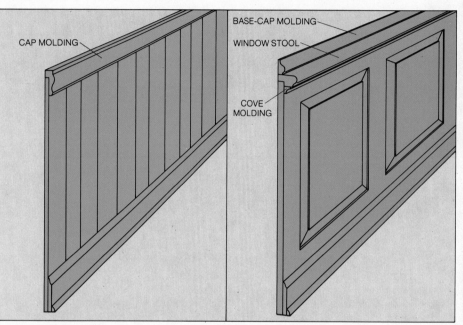

A Coped Joint for a Cap Molding

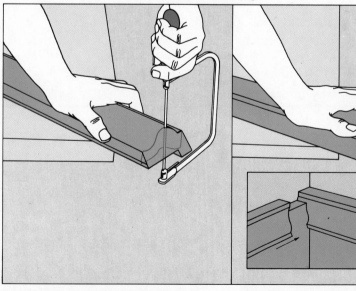

Shaping the ends of the molding. When two pieces of cap molding meet at an inside corner, miter the end of the first piece and outline its contoured edge in pencil (*page 80, Step 1*), but continue the pencil line across the top of the molding, at right angles to the back edge. Using a coping saw, make a vertical cut through the molding along this line (*left*). Then notch the second piece of molding (*right*) deeply enough to allow its lip to slide over the adjoining wainscot (*inset*). Nail the second piece to the wall, then slide the first piece against it.

4 Lowering Ceilings, Doubling Walls

A double barrier against noise. This resilient metal channel is screwed to a ceiling joist only along its narrow, upper edge. When a wallboard ceiling is attached to its lower lip, the channel will bounce sound waves into the air space above, where most of them will dissipate before reaching the fiberglass insulation at the top of the joists. This combination of wallboard, flexible channels, air space, and sound-absorbing insulation is such an effective barrier against noise that even extremely loud shouting below will be almost inaudible in the room above.

Ask almost anyone to define the function of walls and ceilings and the answer you will probably receive is "to divide up a house into rooms." But for a homeowner who is beset by concerns with sound, light, efficient use of space and the high cost of building materials, walls and ceilings must often serve multiple purposes. They may have to act as sound modulators, light reflectors, pipe disguisers, even occasionally as secret storage chambers for valuables or treasured documents. In performing such multiple tasks, one ceiling or wall is, in many cases, simply not enough.

For most homeowners, noise—the endless hum of electrical appliances, blasting of stereos, honking of automobile horns and the roar of jet airplane engines—is the major impetus for installing a double wall or ceiling. Many of these installations involve the use of acoustic tiles and panels, which, like the technology they seek to muffle, are a relatively recent phenomenon in residential interiors; they first appeared just after World War II.

Unlike ceramic tile surfaces, which bounce sound waves in all directions, prefabricated acoustic tile or paneling—stapled directly to an existing ceiling or suspended below it in a metal grid—absorbs sound, much as a sponge absorbs water. As sound waves bounce about inside the fibrous air pockets, a large portion of their energy is transformed into heat. Resilient metal channels and sound-absorbent batt insulation installed behind the tiles or panels can reinforce their soundproofing qualities.

If light is your concern, a layer of light-transmitting plastic panels or louvers, suspended below hidden banks of electrical fixtures mounted on the original ceiling, can bathe an entire room in gentle, even light. Obtrusive pipes and ducts, as well, can disappear behind a smooth expanse of lowered ceiling.

There are other, less pragmatic, reasons for dropping a ceiling or doubling a wall surface, ranging from the purely esthetic to the idiosyncratic. You may be pursuing the charm of artificial wood beams or the secret delights of a wall that harbors an unlikely hiding place. Though history shows that secret hiding places are more firmly rooted in myth than in fact *(page 125),* they do exist and they can be useful. According to FBI records, 50 hostages held by armed bandits in a New York bank made their escape by cutting a hole through a plasterboard wall when their captors fell asleep and fleeing by way of a hidden staircase.

Whatever your reason for constructing these double-surfaced room dividers, they are not difficult to install and they add usefulness to a room. This may be enough to lead you to conclude that two ceilings or walls can be better than one.

Prefabricated Ceilings that Satisfy Special Needs

Though plaster and wallboard are the most common ceiling materials, there are a number of attractive alternatives that offer both special effects and ease of installation. They range from simple embellishments—such as the plaster medallion shown on page 35, which lends character to a plain room—to prefabricated ceiling systems.

These last come in many styles but involve only two basic structural concepts. Either they consist of interlocking tiles that are attached directly to the old ceiling or they are made of floating panels, which are suspended from the ceiling on a lightweight metal grid.

Simplicity, of course, is a major advantage of prefabricated ceiling materials. Because they are precut and already embossed with a decorative finish, they dispense with such preliminaries as mortar mixing or joint taping as well as the final application of paint or wallpaper that other ceiling surfaces require. They also eliminate the cleanup that follows the messiness of wet applications.

Apart from ease of installation, prefabricated ceiling materials offer other advantages. One is sound absorbency. Acoustic tiles or panels, generally made of ½- or ¾-inch fiberboard or noncombustible mineral fiber, absorb 50 to 80 per cent of the sound that would otherwise reverberate through the room (however, these materials have little effect on the flow of sound from one room to another—a problem dealt with on pages 114-121). Before installation, acoustic tiles and panels should be unpacked and allowed to stand for at least 24 hours in the room where they are to be installed so they will become acclimated to the temperature and humidity.

Suspended ceiling panels provide a quick way to resolve the problem of hiding overhead pipes and ducts, as in an unfinished basement. Not only do they block these unsightly elements from view, but the supporting grid can easily be dropped in any one section to cover a particularly low-hanging obstacle. Such an enclosure—known as a break, or soffit—extends below the new ceiling surface only along a section sufficient to hide the obstruction.

If you are working with ceiling tiles, you can create this break by building a wooden frame around the obstacle (page 16), and then fastening tiles to the frame. With a suspended ceiling, you must actually drop a section of grid below the main ceiling level (pages 110-111), a job that will be greatly simplified by the acquisition of two handy tools—a punch for making holes in the necessary hardware and a pop-rivet gun for fastening the sections together.

A suspended ceiling, in addition, can fill a need for shadowless, glare-free overhead lighting. When fluorescent-light fixtures are set into the grid flush with the ceiling, they provide a somewhat more even light than narrow surface-mounted fixtures. In fact, in a situation where more even illumination is desirable—as in a kitchen or recreation room—the basic grid can be used to create a completely luminous ceiling.

For such an installation, fluorescent fixtures are mounted in rows above the grid, and translucent plastic panels replace the acoustic panels. Usually the plastic is flat, with a milk-white or prismatic finish, but luminous ceilings are also available with a wide variety of louvers and other diffusers that alter the quality and quantity of light.

All types of fixtures made for the home commonly use 40-watt deluxe cool-white or warm-white tubes, rather than the institutional-type cool-white tubes, which tend to bleach out warm colors such as red and give the skin a sickly, yellowish hue. Also, to provide the maximum amount of light reflection, the existing ceiling structure above the fixtures—including any exposed joists—is generally painted with two coats of vinyl-based, nonyellowing white paint.

Once you have decided what type of ceiling best suits your needs, you will have to resolve some installation details. First, if you have chosen to use tiles rather than suspended panels, check the condition of the existing ceiling, since this determines your installation technique. If you have a ceiling that is sound and level, you can fasten ceiling tiles directly to the existing surface with brush-on adhesive and staples (first removing any loose paint or wallpaper).

However, you may face a more serious problem—cracked plaster, perhaps, or a ceiling that is not level. In such cases you must first install an intermediate buffer of wood furring strips (pages 11-14). These, rather than the old ceiling, will be the mounting surface for the tiles.

Whatever your choice—tile or suspended ceiling—planning will save you from such mishaps as inadequate lighting or borders of unequal width on opposite sides of the room. The method of calculating borders described in Step 1, opposite, ensures borders of equal and visually pleasing width. As you plan, map your layout on graph paper as a guide for the actual installation.

You should also complete electrical wiring for the ceiling—whether luminous or acoustic—before beginning to install tiles or panel grids. A special extender (page 17) may permit you to bring an existing electrical box down until it is flush with a new tiled ceiling. On the other hand, if you are installing electric fixtures in or behind a suspended ceiling, leave a minimum of 3 inches between the new ceiling and the old to allow for wiring and junction boxes.

The tools required for installing a tile or panel ceiling are minimal. A chalk line is essential for laying down guidelines in the initial planning steps. A pair of tin snips is invaluable for cutting the metal hardware for a suspended ceiling, and lather's nippers—pliers with V-shaped jaws that come together in a long flat surface—are useful for bending the hanging wires you will need.

Stapling Ceiling Tile to Furring Strips

1 Laying out the work. To plan a ceiling tile installation efficiently, you will need to mark off 1-foot intervals along the top of each wall, and at the same time mark the location of any concealed joists, using the method described on page 8. To ensure an even fit across the ceiling, with identically cut tiles at each end of a row, first find the midpoint of a wall and measure from there to the corner. If the distance is an even number of feet plus 3 inches or more, use the midpoint as the starting point in marking off the 1-foot intervals. If the distance is an even number of feet plus less than 3 inches, move the starting point 6 inches to the left or right of the midpoint of the wall.

To calculate the number of tiles needed, count the 1-foot intervals along two adjacent walls; add 1 to each figure, then multiply the two figures. To calculate the number of furring strips needed, count the number of 1-foot intervals along one of the walls that parallel the joists, and add 2 to this figure.

Snap a chalk line across the ceiling between corresponding marks on the two walls running parallel to the joists. Center furring strips over these lines, and nail them to the joists they cross, leveling them as shown in Step 3, page 13. Finally, attach furring strips to the two edges of the ceiling that abut the joists (inset).

2 Installing full tiles. Start the tiling in one corner of the ceiling, using two chalk lines as guides. Snap one chalk line down the center of the next-to-last furring strip from the corner; snap the other at right angles to it, connecting the last pair of 1-foot marks on the two walls that parallel the furring strips. Align the first full tile with the intersection of these lines, tongued edges facing the corner and grooved edges facing the center of the room. Staple through the flanges on the grooved edges into the furring strips.

Slide two additional tiles into place, fitting their tongued edges into the grooved edges of the first tile (inset); make sure that the grooved sides of both new tiles face toward the positions of the next tiles you will install. Then staple through the flanges into the furring strips.

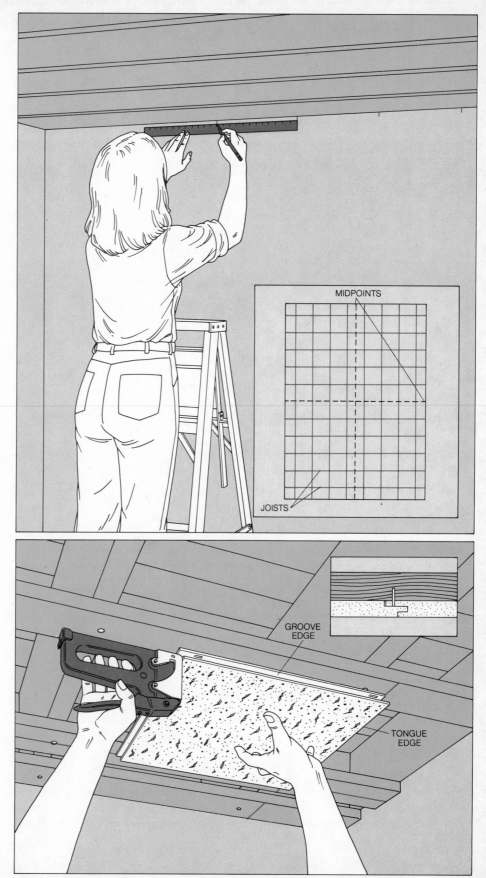

MIDPOINTS

JOISTS

GROOVE EDGE

TONGUE EDGE

105

3 **Adding border tiles.** Cut border tiles to fit spaces between the full tiles and the walls, measuring the border width at both ends of the nearest full tile. Transfer these measurements onto the edges of the corner border tile first—deducting ¼ inch for easy stapling—and cut with a utility knife, using a straightedge guide. In transferring a measurement onto any border tile, measure in from a grooved edge and position the other grooved edge so it faces in the direction you are working.

Slide the border tiles into place, corner tile first, with the cut edges against the wall. Staple the flanged edges of the tiles to furring strips. Fasten them again, with common 1½-inch nails, along the edge against the wall so the nailheads will be covered later by the molding to be installed at the top of the walls. Continue working outward in both directions from the corner, alternately installing full tiles and border tiles as you go.

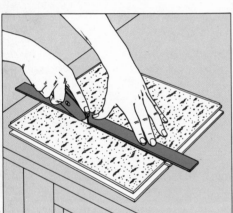

4 **Marking an opening for an outlet box.** Tile as closely as possible to two adjacent sides of an octagonal outlet or junction box; then slip the tongue of a free tile into the groove of an installed tile on one side. Slide the free tile toward the outlet box until it butts against the edge of the box; mark where the midpoint of the box meets the tongue of the tile. Repeat on the adjacent side of the box, moving the tile to mark its other tongued edge in the same way.

With a small L square and a pencil, extend a line from each mark until they intersect; this marks the center of the outlet box. Use a compass to swing from this center a circle slightly smaller than the size of the box.

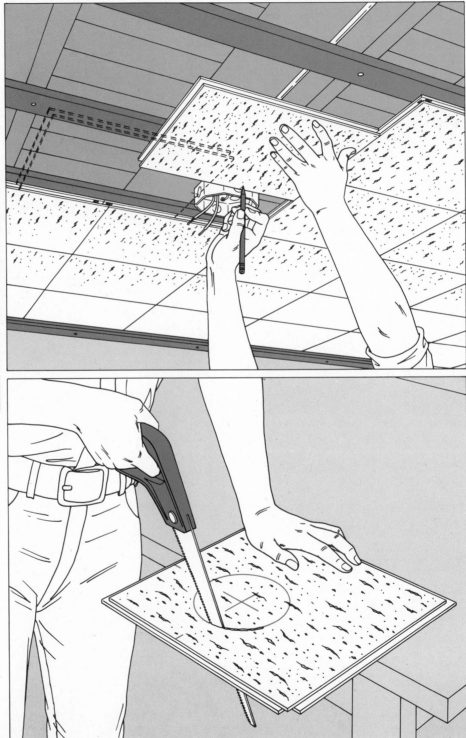

5 **Cutting the outlet-box opening.** With a keyhole or saber-saw blade angled slightly outward, cut a beveled edge around the marked circle. Slide the tile in place over the outlet box and staple it to the furring strips. Continue tiling outward until the entire ceiling is covered.

6 **Attaching ceiling molding.** Cover the edges of the tile and the nailheads along the wall with 1½-inch cove molding. Drive finishing nails through the center of the molding into the wall studs—eightpenny nails are generally sufficient, but use longer nails for heavier molding. For long strips of molding, have a helper steady one end while you attach the other. Trim the molding so it will join snugly at the corners, using the techniques shown on page 80.

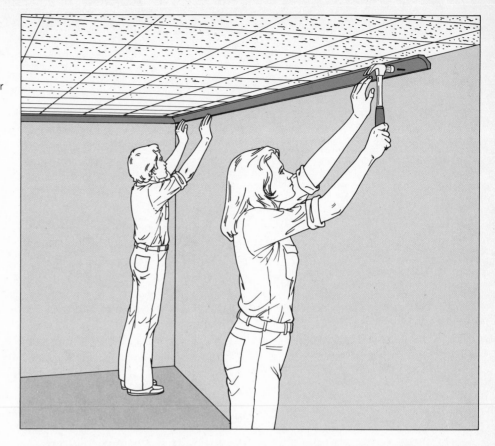

Suspending a Panel Ceiling

1 **Installing the edge framing.** Snap a chalk line across each wall at the desired ceiling height—at least 3 inches below any ducts, pipes or other obstructions—and secure L-shaped edge-framing strips to each wall with nails or screws driven into the studs. Position this framing so the long leg of the L lies against the wall, with the lower leg flush with the chalk line. Lap the ends of adjoining sections over one another at corners (inset) and along the wall.

To plot the positions of runners and cross Ts, first mark the location of any concealed joists (page 8). Then find the midpoint of each wall. On walls that parallel the joists, mark the midpoint at the level of the joist; on walls that run perpendicular to the joists, mark the midpoint just below the bottom of the edge framing.

2 **Laying out the grid.** Mark positions for runners by snapping chalk lines at 2-foot intervals across the ceiling or exposed joists, at right angles to the joists. To determine the position for the first runner, calculate the overage by measuring the number of full feet from the midpoint of the wall to a corner, as in Step 1, page 105. If the overage is 6 inches or more, use the midpoint for the first runner position; if the overage is less than 6 inches, place the first runner 1 foot on either side of the midpoint, and use this position as a reference point for the other chalk lines.

To lay out the positions for cross Ts (*inset*), stretch strings across the ceiling at 4-foot intervals, parallel to the joists and attached just below the bottom of the edge framing. Again determine the position for the first cross T by measuring from a midpoint to a corner to find the overage, but this time note that the overage is calculated from the last foot-mark divisible by 4. If the overage is 6 inches or more, stretch the first string between the midpoints; if it is less than 6 inches, offset the first string 2 feet to one side of the midpoints and use this string as a reference for the remaining strings.

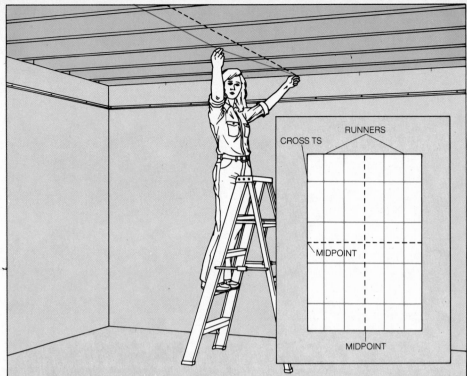

4 **Connecting the cross Ts.** Hook the cross Ts into the runner slots every 2 feet at the locations marked by the strings. Trim the wall ends of the cross Ts with tin snips so that they rest squarely on the edge framing.

3 **Attaching the runners.** Working along the chalk lines, drive an eye screw into every fourth joist and suspend a wire hanger from it, allowing the hanger to extend at least 6 inches below the final ceiling height. Hang the runners from the free ends of the wires by threading the wire through the nearest round hole and twisting the wire with pliers (*inset*). Use the stretched strings as guides to the height of the runners, checking frequently to make sure they are level.

Position the runners so that a slotted hole falls at every string line; trim the runners with a hacksaw, as necessary, to achieve this alignment.

To join sections of runners, butt or snap their ends together, according to the design of the runner hardware. When joining sections, make sure the slots in the added section align with the strings. Trim the ends of the runner so that they rest on the edge framing.

5 **Installing a luminous panel.** With the power turned off, run an electric cable from a junction box to the location you have chosen for the luminous panel and, with a helper, angle the panel into position, resting it on the flanged edges of the runners and the crossed Ts. (To tap into a junction box for this electrical connection, see Step 2, page 110.)

Open the plastic cover of the prewired panel, remove the covering over the wires and ballast, and pull the electric cable through the knock-out hole at the back of the fixture. Secure the cable there with a cable connector and lock nut (*inset*). Use wire caps to connect the black and white cable wires to the corresponding wires on the fixture, and attach the cable ground wire to a grounding screw inside the fixture. Reattach the inside cover over the wires and ballast, insert fluorescent tubes, close the outside cover and turn on the power.

Surround the luminous panels with acoustic panels, angled into position in the same way. At the edges of the ceiling, trim border panels to fit, using a utility knife.

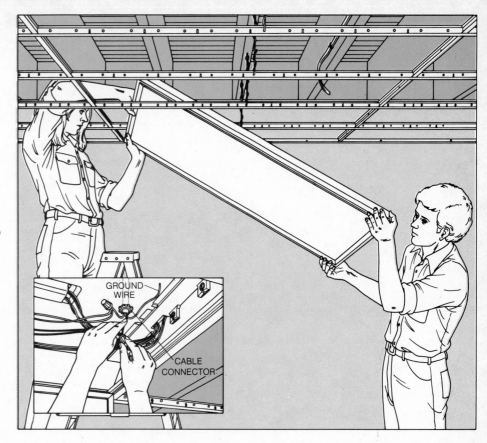

A Luminous Ceiling for Strong, Even Light

1 **Mounting rows of fixtures.** On a finished ceiling, install channel-type fluorescent fixtures, running the length of the room, in rows spaced at about one and a half times the distance between the fixtures and the lowered grid. Measure the length of the room in feet, and divide by 4 to find how many 48-inch standard-sized fixtures you can install in each row. Allow 6 or 8 inches between the wall and the first and last rows.

Hold the first fixture in place and mark its mounting holes. Drill holes for screws. Use screw anchors if the ceiling is only plaster or wallboard; at joists, no special anchors are needed. Knock out the tabs in the connector holes at the ends of the fixture and mount it.

Butt the second fixture against the first, mark its mounting holes and install it. Join the fixtures with connector studs and lock nuts (*inset*). Install and join the remaining fixtures.

If the ceiling has exposed joists, snap chalk lines and install the fixtures perpendicular to the joists. Or mount the fixtures in the spaces between the joists. The method depends on the proposed height for the finished ceiling.

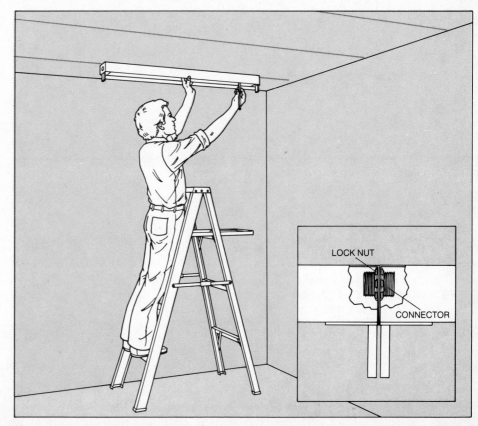

2 Tapping into a junction box. With the power turned off, run lengths of specially insulated cable, called THHN cable, from one end of each row of fixtures to an existing or newly mounted junction box, fastening the cables to the ceiling or the joists with cable staples. Put the cables through knockout holes in the junction boxes and secure them with cable connectors and lock nuts. Then connect the cables to the house wiring with wire caps, matching black wires to black, white to white and bare ground wire to bare ground wire and to the box *(inset)*.

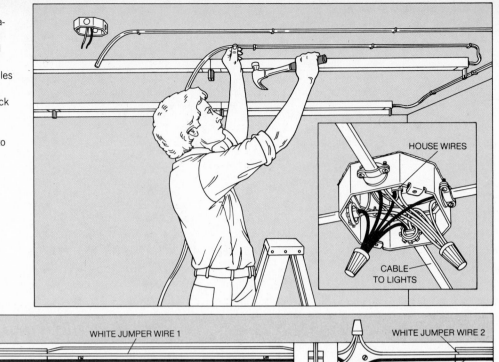

HOUSE WIRES

CABLE TO LIGHTS

WHITE FIXTURE WIRE   WHITE JUMPER WIRE 1   WHITE JUMPER WIRE 2

GROUNDING SCREW   BLACK FIXTURE WIRE   BLACK JUMPER WIRE 1   BLACK JUMPER WIRE 2

3 Wiring the fixtures. With the power still turned off, use cable connectors to connect the free ends of the cables to the first of the fixtures in each row. Use a wire cap to connect the black cable wire to its corresponding wire in the fixture and to a length of black wire, called a jumper wire, long enough to reach into the second fixture in the row. Then connect the white wires in the same manner, adding a white wire long enough to reach into the second fixture. At-

tach the bare cable wire to the grounding screw in the first fixture.

Run the connecting wires into the second fixture through the channel provided for that purpose, and attach them to the corresponding wires in that fixture, again adding connecting wires long enough to reach into the third fixture. Continue in this fashion until all the fixtures in each row are hooked up. Then replace the covers over

the wiring and ballast in each fixture, install a 40-watt, rapid-start fluorescent tube and turn on the power to check the installation.

For the luminous ceiling, install the metal grid of runners and cross Ts as for an acoustic ceiling *(Steps 1 through 4, pages 107-108)*. Slide the panels into place, trimming border panels to size. To cut a plastic panel, score it a few times with a utility knife and snap on the scored line.

Boxing In Obstructions

1 Installing a dropped runner. When an obstruction runs parallel to the runners on the main part of the ceiling, install the main grid as close as possible to both sides of the obstruction *(pages 107-109)*. Then attach hanger wires directly beneath the last main runner on both sides of the obstruction, cutting the wires so that the dropped runners will lie at least 3 inches below the obstruction. If the dropped runners butt against a wall, attach a piece of edge framing to the wall for support. Then attach the runners to the hanger wires *(Step 3, page 108)*, aligning the slots for the cross Ts.

If an obstruction runs perpendicular to the runners on the main ceiling, cut the main runners on both sides of the obstruction, leaving a 2-foot gap between them for cross Ts. Then install dropped runners as described above.

PIPE

HANGER WIRE

NEW CEILING

RUNNERS

2 **Attaching supports for side panels.** Prepare
U-shaped channel molding to support the top of
the side panels by holding the molding upside
down against the bottom of the main runner nearest the obstruction. Punch holes through the
molding and the inner edge of the runner, spacing
the holes about 18 to 24 inches apart. Or drill
holes through the molding, then hold the molding
against the runner to mark the hole positions,
and drill matching holes in the runner. Use a pop-
rivet gun and the fasteners known as pop rivets to
fasten the molding to the runner.

In like manner, fashion a support for the bottom of
the side panels by fastening an L-shaped wall
angle to the bottom of both dropped runners,
positioning the wall angle so that the space
between the spine of the runner and the upright of
the L is just wide enough to accommodate the
bottom of the panel—usually ½ to ¾ inch (inset).
If the enclosure does not extend all the way
across the room, provide similar supports for the
top and bottom of the panel that frames the end
of the enclosure.

Connect cross Ts to the two dropped runners
at 4-foot intervals (Step 4, page 108). Insert
acoustic panels into the grid this creates.

3 **Installing side panels.** Cut 2-by-4-foot acoustic
panels to fit the height of the enclosure and install them, framing the joint between panels with
a cross T cut to fit snugly between the wall angle on the dropped runner and the channel molding on the ceiling runner (inset). Insert each
panel by angling it up into the channel molding,
then letting it drop into the wall angle. As each
panel is installed, add a vertical cross T, then another panel, until the obstruction is enclosed.
If the vertical cross Ts need steadying, you can
pop-rivet or screw them to the runners.

To provide a neat corner trim on an enclosure that
does not extend across the room, fit sections
of L molding over the corner and attach the molding to the upper and lower runners.

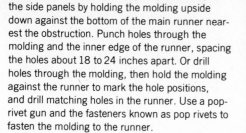

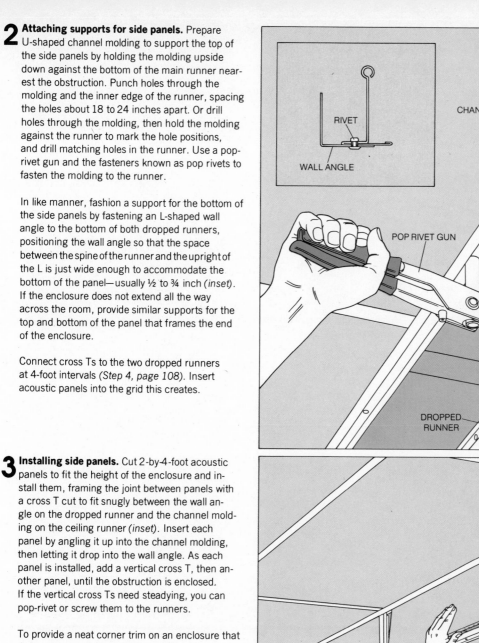

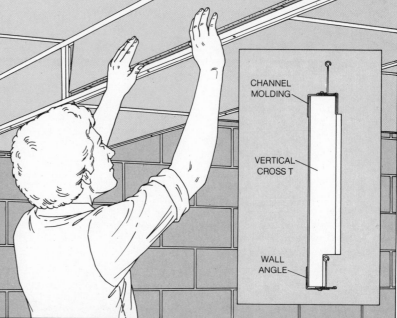

An Easy Way to Simulate a Beamed Ceiling

You can achieve the aura of antiquity that exposed ceiling beams lend to a room without resorting to major structural changes and without hoisting any heavy timbers. The "beams" shown here are constructed of 1-inch lumber, which is actually only ¾ inch thick; they are lightweight and hollow, and once assembled can be finished to resemble whatever decorative style you prefer.

You might choose to bevel the beams and stain them dark in the fashion of Tudor England; you might roughen and gouge them, in imitation of the hand-hewn beams of pioneer America; or you may decide to leave them smooth and paint them with running designs in the tradition of North European peasant art.

The arrangement of the beams across the ceiling is also a matter of personal preference. Although simulated beams generally parallel each other across the width of a room, supported by the existing joists, you can, if you like, add cross beams placed at right angles between long beams. You can even add posts along the walls beneath the ends of the beams and, as a final touch, add bracing beams at 45° angles, running them from the posts to the ceiling beams.

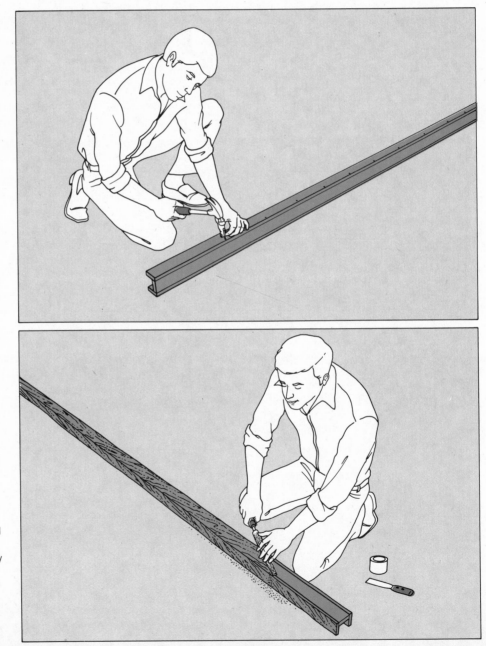

1 **Building the beam.** Make a hollow U-shaped beam by gluing and nailing together three 1-by-4s or three 1-by-6s, using sixpenny finishing nails. Be sure to position the sidepieces so their edges lie precisely flush with the bottom piece, resulting in an almost invisible joint. If you work with a soft wood such as pine, nailing the pieces together will help straighten slight warps and twists. Countersink the nails; then, if you are going to paint the beams, fill the nail holes and any noticeable joints with wood putty.

2 **Applying the decorative finish.** For a rough-hewn look, scrape the beam with a rasp or wire brush. You can further distress the wood by hitting it with a chain or a ring of old keys. Finally, apply a wood stain if you want to darken the wood. For a Tudor or Early American beam, bevel the edges of the sidepieces with a block plane, a rasp or sandpaper, then apply a dark mahogany or walnut stain followed by polyurethane varnish. For a beam with painted decorations, sand the unstained wood and add the decorative design of your choice, using a stencil or painting the design freehand. When the paint is dry, finish the beam with polyurethane varnish.

3 **Installing the mounting tracks.** Attach boards as mounting tracks along the ceiling where the beams will go, using 2-by-4 tracks for beams made of 1-by-4s, and 2-by-6 tracks for 1-by-6 beams. With 16-penny common nails, fasten the tracks across ceiling joists, which usually are spaced at 16-inch intervals, center to center. Use a magnetic stud finder to locate joists and verify by drilling small holes. If the beams run parallel to and between joists, fasten the tracks to the ceiling with toggle bolts every 2 feet.

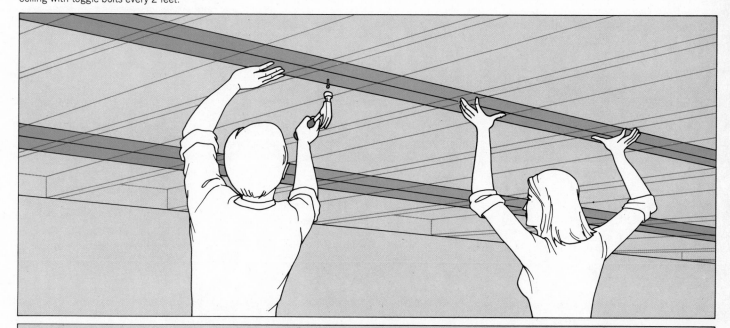

4 **Mounting the beam.** With a helper, slide the beam into position over its mounting track, pressing it firmly against the ceiling. Drive six-penny finishing nails at 1-foot intervals through the sidepieces of the beam and into the mounting track, and countersink the heads. Then, if you are painting the beams, cover the nailheads with wood putty first; if you stain the beams, apply matching wood putty afterward.

To install short cross beams, fasten each track to the ceiling with toggle bolts and toenail it to the adjacent long beams. Install the short lengths of U-shaped beams as described above.

Blocking Noise to Make a House More Livable

One important function of walls and ceilings is to block sound, and there are several ways to do it. Soundproofing a room may be as simple as sealing gaps around a door, or it may require rebuilding an entire wall or lowering a ceiling. The precise solution, however, can be maddeningly elusive, because noise not only travels directly through the air, but penetrates readily through solids like walls, studs and ceiling joists. To make matters worse, sound can turn corners and penetrate tiny cracks with relatively little loss in intensity.

To create an effective sound barrier, you must block airborne sound, interrupt the path of sound transmitted through solids, and plug acoustic leaks. Fortunately, the mechanics of dealing with all three are relatively simple. Sound is the pulsing movement of air molecules against the eardrum. When a vibrating surface—such as the cone of a loudspeaker or the human vocal cords—disturbs the air in a room, it sets up a wave pattern of molecular motion. Bumping against one another, the displaced air molecules transmit acoustic energy, rath-

er as gelatin transmits a shudder, until the motion reaches the eardrums.

Any barrier that interferes with this motion reduces sound, and generally the denser the barrier the smaller the amount of sound that will penetrate. A brick wall 4 inches thick is a far better sound barrier than the conventional 2-by-4 stud wall. But unfortunately, a solid wall thick enough to reduce sound significantly would be entirely too heavy for a room partition.

Nor does it help much to increase the density of a conventional 2-by-4 stud wall by simply adding extra layers of wallboard or by blowing insulation between the studs—two common approaches to soundproofing. Often the wallboard continues to pick up sound vibrations and pass them through the solid 2-by-4 studs, setting in motion the equally flexible wallboard on the other side. Similarly, acoustic tiles—which are very effective at absorbing sound within a room—do little or nothing to prevent the transmission of sound from room to room since sound passes right through their lightweight, porous composition.

The best way to obstruct the movement of sound through a wall is to isolate the wall surfaces from the wall studs. One way to do this is with resilient metal channels made especially for this purpose. Attached to the edges of wood studs and joists, these thin metal strips, only ½ inch deep, are flexible enough to absorb and dissipate most of the vibration in the wall surface, much as a spring damps mechanical vibration.

Resilient channels work, however, only when there is at least 2 inches of air space between the two wall surfaces. If you attach them to an existing wall or ceiling and then top them with a new surface only ½ inch away, they will indeed dampen the structural transmission of sound, but so much vibration will pass directly through the narrow air space from one surface to the other that most of the effectiveness of the channel will be wasted.

If you do want to install a new sound barrier directly over an old one, use Z furring channels instead. These springy metal strips, Z-shaped in cross section *(page 117)*, behave like large resilient

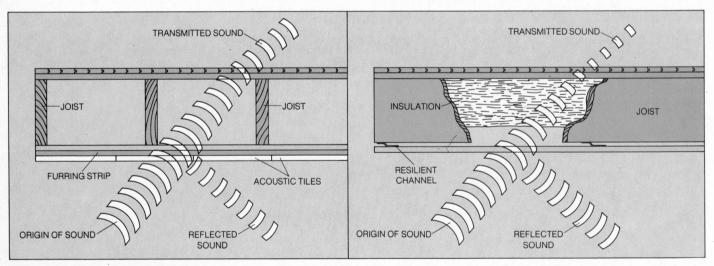

Sound absorption and transmission. Porous acoustic tiles covering a ceiling *(left)* reduce the noise within a room by absorbing airborne sound. But they do little to stop sound transmission through partitions into adjacent rooms. A wallboard ceiling that rides on resilient channels and has insulation between joists *(right)* does not dampen sound within a room, but significantly reduces sound transmitted to the room above.

channels, but are deep enough to separate the two surfaces sufficiently.

When you stop the structural transmission of sound, you make the air within the wall a much less effective medium for transmitting noise. But you can, if you like, block the sound even more by filling the wall with standard home insulation. Insulation fibers act like tiny springs, absorbing acoustic energy as well as blocking heat transmission.

In new construction the same principles of sound control apply, but with the advantage that they can be built into the structure from the beginning. The 2-by-6 staggered-stud wall—which has two separate rows of studs staggered on 2-by-6 plates *(page 120)*—interrupts the transmission of sound between two rooms effectively enough to render loud speech barely audible. Even shouting can scarcely be heard through the double 2-by-4 wall *(page 121),* with two entirely separate frames; and this wall is also good at reducing pulsing bass tones.

Ceilings, by and large, respond to the same sound-deadening treatments as walls, with one exception. Impact noise—intense, localized sounds like those of high heels rapping on the floor overhead—presents special problems. Resilient channels on the ceiling joists will eliminate some of this vertical sound but usually you will also have to install a padded carpet over walking areas.

The best of these sound barriers may prove inadequate, however, if sound vibrations can skirt the wall, moving under, over or around it. Sound may travel from one room to another along an unfinished attic floor, for instance, or a crawl space or ventilating duct. Before starting any soundproofing construction, make sure that these pathways can be blocked—and that the task is worth the effort.

You may be able to reduce sound travel through ducts by gluing 1-inch-thick neoprene-coated duct lining to the inside walls of the duct *(page 121).* If this is not enough, ducts may have to be taken apart and fitted with elaborate baffles.

Much easier to deal with are holes and cracks in the wall itself, which can leak a surprising amount of noise. A crack just ⅛ inch wide and 8 inches long can reduce the effectiveness of a soundproof wall by as much as 10 per cent. As a first step, caulk all perimeter joints in the wall with acoustic sealant, a caulking compound that never hardens. If necessary, remove the baseboard to caulk the joint along the floor.

Block cracks around doors by installing oval neoprene gaskets *(page 121).* Even a hollow-core door, which is a poor sound barrier, can be improved somewhat by perimeter gaskets. In homes with central heating, interior doors sometimes cannot be sealed, since the heating system—and its return registers—may depend on the circulation of air under doors.

Other acoustic leaks, more difficult to detect, are those that occur when electrical or telephone outlets are set back-to-back in adjacent rooms. To plug these leaks, you will have to relocate the outlets so they are separated by at least the width of one stud cavity. Then caulk around the fixtures with acoustic sealant and insulate the space between them with fiberglass.

Most of the tools and materials you will need for these soundproofing projects—from building a double wall to plugging a hole—are sold at building-supply stores, although in some areas neoprene gaskets may have to be ordered from stores specializing in weatherproofing materials. Because screws are better than nails for installing resilient channels, it generally pays to rent an electric screw gun, or to buy a screwdriving attachment for a variable-speed electric drill.

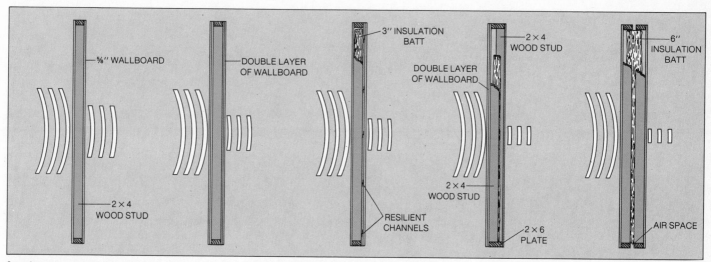

A variety of sound barriers. The sound-stopping capabilities of these five walls are determined by a combination of factors: the overall thickness of the wall, the density and rigidity of the surface material, and the nature of the contact between surface and support.

The standard 2-by-4 stud wall *(far left),* covered with one layer of ⅝-inch gypsum wallboard, renders ordinary conversation in an adjacent room audible but unintelligible. With a second layer of ⅝-inch wallboard added *(near left),* loud speech can be heard but usually not understood. A better result is achieved with only one layer of wallboard when resilient channels are added to one wall *(center),* and a 3-inch-thick layer of insulation is installed between studs. You can block both structural and airborne sound transmission dramatically by separating and staggering the placement of opposite 2-by-4 studs on 2-by-6 plates and adding two wallboard layers *(near right).* More effective still is the double 2-by-4 wall *(far right).* With two pairs of sole and top plates set 1 inch apart, plus a 6-inch layer of insulation between studs, and a layer of wallboard on each side, this hollow double wall stops sound better than a 4-inch solid brick wall.

Soundproofing
an Existing Wall

1 **Attaching resilient channels.** Remove the existing wall surface, exposing the studs, and fill the space between the studs with 3½-inch-thick batts of fiberglass insulation. For an exterior wall, the vapor-barrier backing of the batts should face toward the room; for an interior wall, no vapor barrier is necessary. Then fasten rows of resilient channel across the studs, wide flange up; use 1¼-inch dry-wall screws, one screw per stud. Position the top row of channel 6 inches below the ceiling, the bottom row 2 inches above the floor. Space intervening rows evenly at intervals of about 20 inches—but no more than 24 inches apart. When joining lengths of channel to span a long wall, overlap the ends 2 inches (*inset*) and put the joint at a stud.

Be sure when removing plaster or wallboard, and when handling fiberglass, to keep the room well ventilated and to wear a respirator and gloves. Pry out any nails left in the studs and add box extenders (*page 17*) to electrical outlets, to allow for the ½-inch depth of the channels plus the two layers of ½-inch wallboard.

2 **Mounting the floating wall.** Install the first layer of wallboard vertically, leaving a ⅛-inch clearance all around—between panels and at ceiling and floor. Shim the panels to hold them off the floor until they are screwed into place. Secure the panels to the resilient channels with 1-inch dry-wall screws inserted at 24-inch intervals. Caulk the ⅛-inch gap around the panels with acoustic sealant (*inset*).

Install the second layer of wallboard horizontally, using 1⅝-inch dry-wall screws to fasten them to the underlying channels; space the screws 16 inches apart. As before, leave a ⅛-inch gap between panels and at ceiling and floor, and caulk the gaps with acoustic sealant. Cover joints between panels with tape and joint compound as shown on pages 23-25.

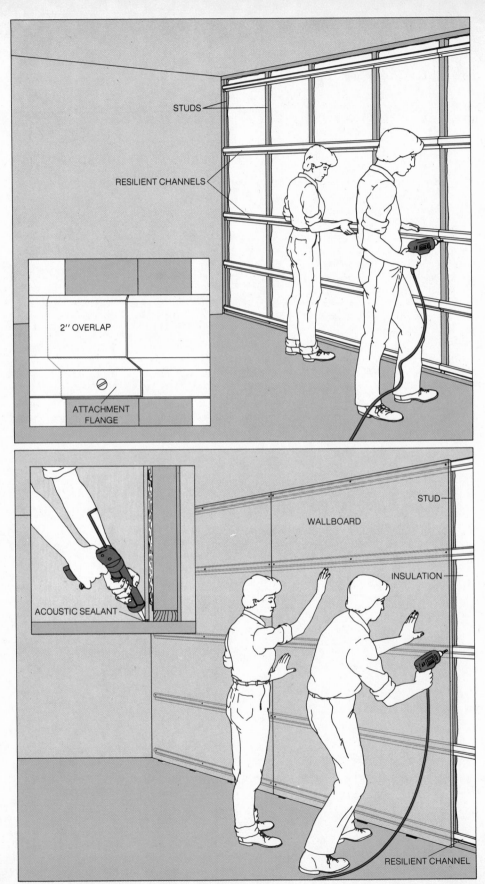

STUDS

RESILIENT CHANNELS

2" OVERLAP

ATTACHMENT FLANGE

ACOUSTIC SEALANT

STUD

WALLBOARD

INSULATION

RESILIENT CHANNEL

A Freestanding Wall to Buffer Sound

Cross section of a false wall. This metal-stud wall, erected with the sole plate 2 inches out from an existing wall, is assembled as shown on pages 62 and 63. The space between walls and the inherent resiliency of the metal studs are dual barriers to structure-borne sound. In addition, the spaces between studs are filled with 3½-inch batts of fiberglass insulation to reduce airborne sound. The wallboard surface of the new wall, installed ⅛ inch away from adjacent surfaces, is caulked with acoustic sealant.

Covered with a single layer of ⅝-inch wallboard, this freestanding wall effectively reduces the transmission of even low-pitched sounds. However, if the sound is extreme—such as that produced by an electric bass guitar—you might further reduce noise transmission by removing the surface from the original wall, and filling the additional air space with insulation.

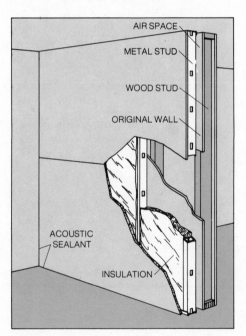

Adding a Layer to the Existing Ceiling

Attaching the Z-shaped channels. Locate and mark the joist positions as shown on page 12. Then mark the position for the first two rows of Z channel by snapping chalk lines 6 inches out from the two walls running perpendicular to the joists. Divide and mark the intervening space evenly for the rest of the rows, with the rows 20 to 24 inches apart.

Fasten 2-inch-deep Z channel across the joists with 1½-inch dry-wall screws, making sure that all the flanged edges face in the same direction; use one screw at each joist.

When you are joining lengths of channel, overlap the channel ends 2 inches and fasten them to the joist with the same screw.

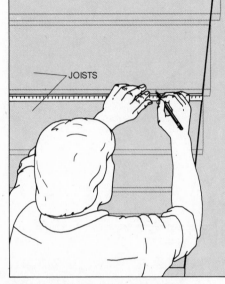
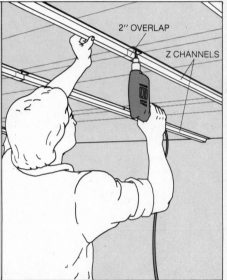

Adding wallboard and insulation. When all the Z channels are in place, install the first row of wallboard paneling across them and insert 2-inch batts of fiberglass insulation between the wallboard and the existing ceiling. When installing the wallboard, leave a ⅛-inch gap between the panel edges and the adjacent walls, and secure the panels to the channels with 1-inch dry-wall screws set at 12-inch intervals. If more than one panel is needed to span the ceiling, center the joint between panels over a channel, and use two screws to fasten them to the channel (*inset*). For a smooth seam at such joints, install the wallboard in the direction opposite to the direction of the lower flange and secure the screw nearest the flange edge first; this ensures that the flange will remain horizontal.

When the first row of wallboard is in place, install the remaining rows, one at a time, each time filling the space between the wallboard and the existing ceiling with insulation batts. Butt the edges of the panels together and on the last row, glue the insulation batt to the back of the panel before installing it. Caulk all of the ⅛-inch gaps with acoustic sealant. Finish the seams between panels with tape and joint compound, as shown on pages 23-25.

Rebuilding the Existing Ceiling from Scratch

1 **Creating space for insulation.** Remove the existing ceiling, observing the same precautions as in removing a wall *(page 11)*, and install 6-inch-thick batts of fiberglass insulation, vapor barrier facing downward, between the exposed joists. Staple the batts to the sides of the joists, about one third of the way up the joist. If you wish to extend an electrical box, see page 17.

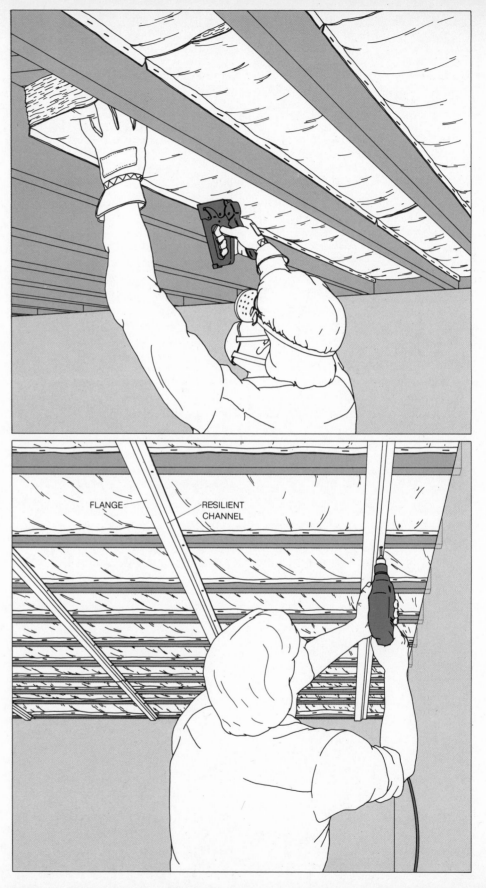

FLANGE

RESILIENT CHANNEL

2 **Attaching resilient channels.** Install resilient channels across the exposed joists, spacing them as for Z channels *(page 117)*. Use 1¼-inch dry-wall screws, one screw per joist, and make sure all the channel flanges run in the same direction. When joining two channels end-to-end, overlap sections of channel by 2 inches and join them together at a joist.

Fasten wallboard panels across the resilient channels, working against the direction of the flanges *(page 117)*. Leave a ⅛-inch gap around the perimeter of the ceiling. If you need to join two panels in order to span a ceiling, center their joint over a channel, and fasten them to the channel as shown on page 117. Caulk all the gaps with an acoustic sealant, and finish the seams between panels as described on pages 23-25.

Using Staggered Studs to Muffle Noise

1 Locating the top and sole plates. For a wall running perpendicular to joists, snap two chalk lines across the ceiling 5½ inches apart, to mark for a 2-by-6 top plate. Drop a plumb bob from several points along one line, mark the floor, and draw a guideline for the sole plate.

For a wall running parallel to the joists, center the top plate directly under a joist, if possible. Determine the location of the joist *(page 8)* and drive a nail partway into the center of it at each side of the room. Snap a chalk line between the two nails to mark the center of the top plate *(right)*, then outline the plate with two additional chalk lines, parallel to the center line and 5½ inches apart. Drop a plumb bob from several points, as before, to mark the position of the edge of the sole plate.

If the wall must stand between parallel joists, cut away enough of the ceiling to expose the two joists flanking the wall. Install blocking of the same size lumber as the joists, every 2 feet *(inset, right)*, toenailing the blocks in place. Fill the spaces between the blocks with fiberglass. Patch the ceiling *(pages 22-23)*, then locate the top and sole plates for the new wall as for a wall running perpendicular to the joists.

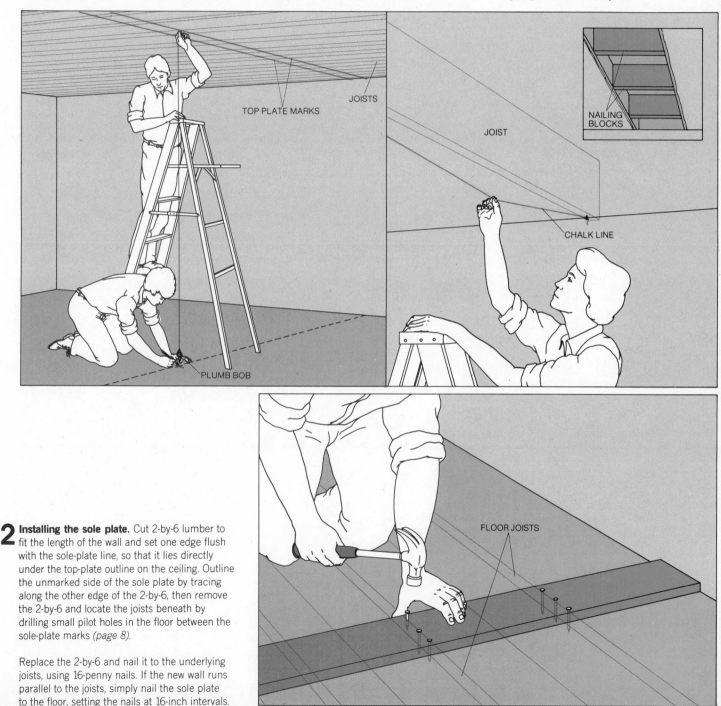

TOP PLATE MARKS

JOISTS

PLUMB BOB

JOIST

CHALK LINE

NAILING BLOCKS

FLOOR JOISTS

2 Installing the sole plate. Cut 2-by-6 lumber to fit the length of the wall and set one edge flush with the sole-plate line, so that it lies directly under the top-plate outline on the ceiling. Outline the unmarked side of the sole plate by tracing along the other edge of the 2-by-6, then remove the 2-by-6 and locate the joists beneath by drilling small pilot holes in the floor between the sole-plate marks *(page 8)*.

Replace the 2-by-6 and nail it to the underlying joists, using 16-penny nails. If the new wall runs parallel to the joists, simply nail the sole plate to the floor, setting the nails at 16-inch intervals.

3 **Marking the plates for studs.** Mark each end of the sole plate for a 2-by-6 stud, then mark along one edge of the plate for 2-by-4 studs spaced 24 inches on center, with their edges flush with that edge of the sole plate. On the opposite edge of the sole plate, mark a second row of stud positions, staggered midway between the first row. Then lay the 2-by-6 top plate beside the sole plate and, using a carpenter's square, transfer the marks to the top plate.

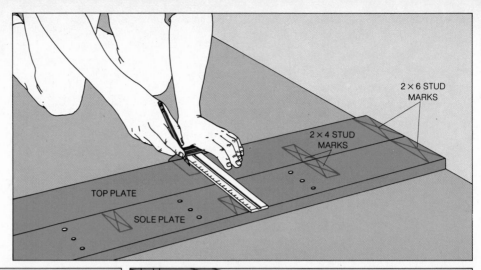

2 × 6 STUD MARKS

2 × 4 STUD MARKS

TOP PLATE

SOLE PLATE

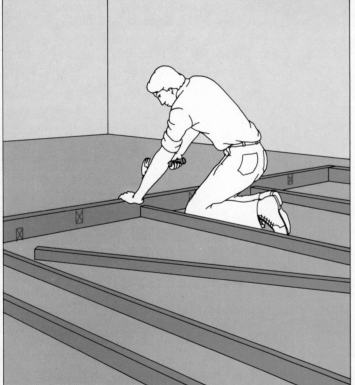

4 **Assembling the framework.** Measure the height of the ceiling, subtract the combined thickness of the sole and top plates, and cut 2-by-4 studs to this length. With the top plate lying on edge, nail one row of studs along the lower edge of the plate. Then nail 2-by-6 studs, cut to the same length, to each end of the plate. With a helper, raise the assembly onto the sole plate, and nail the top plate to the ceiling joist or joists. If the joists run perpendicular to the partition, nail end studs to the walls only if there is a wall stud to nail to. Line up the studs with the marks on the sole plate, and toenail them in place with 10-penny nails, two nails on one side, a third on the other. Toenail the remaining studs to the other edge of the plates.

5 **Completing the wall.** Insert fiberglass insulation batts, 3½ inches thick and 24 inches wide, vertically between the studs on one side of the wall. Then cover both sides of the wall with a double layer of ½-inch wallboard, leaving ⅛-inch of clearance around the perimeter of the wall. Caulk the ⅛-inch gaps with acoustic sealant, and finish the seams between sheets of wallboard with tape and joint compound as on pages 23-25.

A Double Wall to Stop Low-pitched Sound

Constructing the two walls. Mark positions on the floor and ceiling for two sole plates and two top plates, 1 inch apart, using the same technique as in laying out the staggered-stud wall *(Steps 1 and 2, page 119)*, but use 2-by-4 plates, and space the studs 16 inches on center—it is not necessary to stagger the studs. Assemble and install one frame as for the staggered-stud wall *(Step 4, opposite);* cover its outer surface with a double layer of ½-inch wallboard *(Step 2, page 116).*

Erect the second frame in the same way, but insert 6-inch-thick fiberglass insulation batts between its studs before covering it with the double layer of wallboard. Caulk perimeter gaps with acoustic sealant and finish seams with tape and joint compound *(pages 23-25).*

Plugging Acoustic Leaks

Muffling an air duct. Remove the register grilles and measure as far into the duct as your arms will reach. Cut four pieces of 1-inch-thick neoprene-coated duct liner to this length, and as wide as the dimensions of the interior walls of the duct. Seal the cut edges of the liner with a coating of duct-liner adhesive or contact cement to prevent glass fibers in the cut edge from blowing into the air. Working one piece at a time, spread duct-liner adhesive on the rough, uncoated side of the liner and press it into place on the duct wall. Line remaining sides of the interior of the duct in the same manner. Then replace the grille.

Sealing cracks around doors. Cut oval neoprene gasket the length of the door frame and test-fit by holding the gasket against the door frame—the gasket should compress slightly when the door is closed, without interfering with the latch. When the gasket fits correctly, mark the screw holes along its aluminum mount. Drill holes and fasten the gasket in place.

On the bottom of the door, measure the gap between door and threshold. Typically, 5/16 inch is the clearance needed for a bottom gasket. If there is no threshold, install an aluminum sill 7/16 inch high. Trim the bottom of the door accordingly when you remove it to install the gasket. Rehang the door and test the gasket by sliding a credit card along the bottom of the door, between the gasket and the threshold; the card should meet slight resistance.

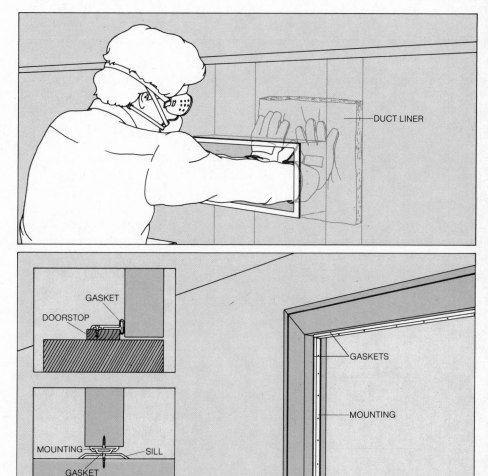

Secret Hiding Places in Walls and Ceilings

Secret spaces behind walls and ceilings are usually associated with mystery movies and the mansions of eccentric millionaires. But in fact the nooks and crannies left within the framework of a conventional house can be handy places to hide family treasures—provided these are not so valuable as to be better off in a safe-deposit box. A bookcase, seemingly as stable as the wall to which it is attached, can swing open to reveal a cubbyhole, or a closet ceiling can tilt up to disclose an unsuspected recess.

The location of such hiding places must naturally be limited to interior wall areas free of ducts, wires or pipes, but it is not necessarily restricted in size to the standard 3½-inch width of a stud wall. If you can mount a bookcase on a wall beneath a staircase, or against a wall with a closet on the far side, you can have a secret storage area of considerable size.

A false ceiling can simply rest on a ledge of crown molding but a swinging bookcase must be fitted with special hinges, called pivot hinges. These are nearly but not completely invisible; therefore the hinges should be mounted so that the edges of the recessed hardware are above and below eye level, where they are less conspicuous. The hinges, which have an odd shape and an intricate mounting procedure, are made in sizes that will support as much as 150 pounds. Even so, it is better to keep weight on the bookcase to a minimum, using the shelves for knickknacks and photographs rather than heavy books.

The bookcase itself must be sturdily constructed of at least ¾-inch lumber, rabbetted at the joints. It needs a strong back and, if one is not there already, an added 1-by-2 horizontal brace along the inside juncture of the top and back. A bookcase 32 inches wide fits conveniently across three studs, but it can be virtually any size or shape, limited only by the dimensions of the recess behind it and the weight that it must bear.

A Hidden Recess behind a Bookcase

Creating the cavity. This typical wall opening, made by cutting away wallboard or plaster and lath, stretches from the center of one stud to the center of another, 32 inches away. Thin plywood panels, glued to the lath or wallboard of the wall behind, provide a back. Thicker boards line the sides of studs, serving as supports for the two middle shelves. The bottom shelves rest on cleats so that their surfaces are flush with the cut in the wall. At the top, the recess is closed off with two boards the same size as shelves; they are installed by first nailing them to their supports, forming inverted Us. Then the three-piece assemblies are slipped into place and nailed to the studs. The edge of the opening is smoothed with spackle or adhesive joint tape.

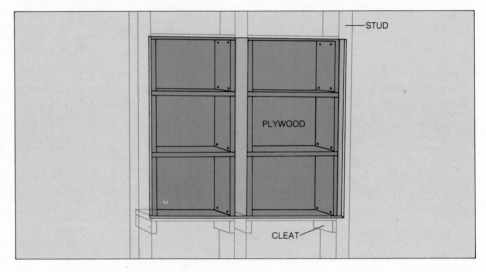

How to Suspend the Bookcase

1 Mortising for the hinges. Outline the shape of the movable leaf of the hinge on the top of the bookcase, positioning the hinge ¼ inch in from the side of the bookcase. Using a wood chisel and mallet, cut a mortise for the hinge only as deep as the thickness of the steel from which the hinge is made. Repeat at the bottom of the bookcase. Screw both hinges onto the bookcase—but only through the elongated holes.

While a helper holds the bookcase in position against the recess, mark for the stationary leaves of the hinges on the supporting studs; also mark the position of the screw holes. Lower the bookcase; unscrew the hinges from the top and bottom of the bookcase and screw them to the studs through the elongated holes.

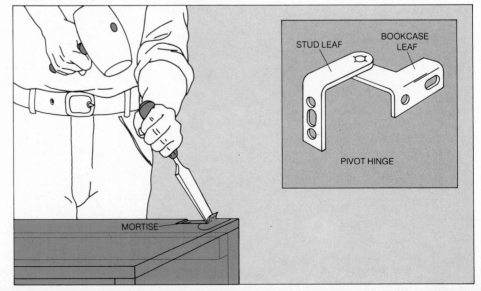

2 **Mounting the bookcase.** While a helper holds the bookcase against them, test and adjust the positions of the hinges on the stud. Then drive screws through all screw holes in the stationary leaves of the hinges and, with the helper still supporting the bookcase, drive screws through the elongated holes on the back of the movable leaf, into the back of the bookcase. Open and close the bookcase to check for proper action of the hinges (inset), making adjustments as necessary. When the bookcase closes neatly against the recess, drive screws through all the remaining holes in the hinges.

Attach thin strips of wood, felt or rubber to the stud against which the bookcase closes, so that the latching side of the bookcase protrudes from the studs as much as the hinged side.

3 **Disguising the joint with molding.** Cut four sections of ⅜-inch door or window molding to fit around the recess. Notch the top and bottom sections to fit around the horizontal parts of the hinges, and miter all the ends. Tack the molding around the recess and try closing the bookcase; if its back hits the edge of the molding, use a block plane to shave away some of the wood at the edges of the bookcase until it slips snugly into the molding. Then nail the molding permanently to the wall.

Note: Move the molding itself only if its alignment is obviously wrong—moving it too much will leave a visible gap between the molding and the bookcase when the bookcase is closed.

4 **Securing the bookcase with a catch.** Screw the double-roller half of a spring-action catch to the stud framing one side of the recess, positioning the catch so that the rollers lie flush with the opening. Then swing the bookcase nearly closed and mark on its side a line where the two rollers intersect. Mount the latching half of the catch on the back of the bookcase at the height of the mark (inset, near right, top). Open and close the bookcase and, if necessary, reposition the double-roller half forward or backward to hold the bookcase closed tightly against the wall (inset, near right, bottom).

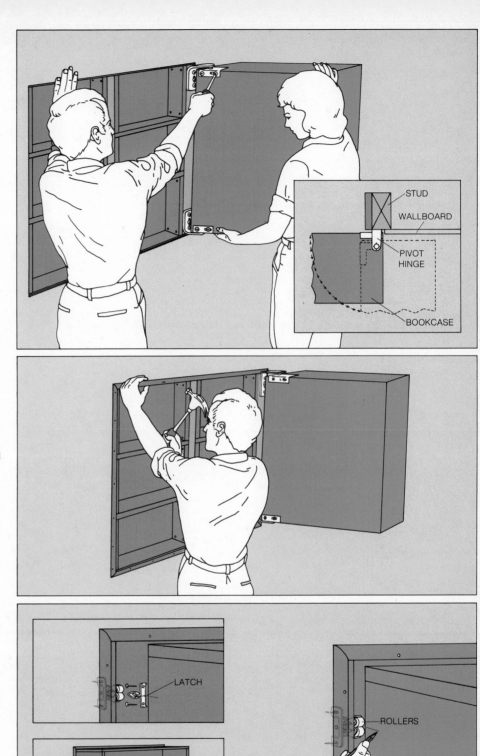

A False Ceiling to Hide Shelves in a Closet

1 **Putting up the molding.** Measure at least 4 inches up from the molding on the top of the closet door and construct a storage area, cutting away wallboard and installing shelves as on page 122; then cut mitered lengths of crown or rake molding to fit the perimeter of the closet. Fasten the molding to the wall with panel adhesive and with nails driven into all the studs, including those at the corners. Then drive nails at a slight angle into the wallboard halfway between the studs to hold the molding securely in place until the adhesive sets.

2 **Installing the false ceiling.** Cut a piece of plywood and a piece of wallboard ½ inch smaller than the width and length of the closet. Nail the wallboard panel to the plywood backing with twopenny finishing nails spaced every 6 inches along the edge, and cover the nailheads (*page 24, Step 3*). Tilt the wallboard panel into place, resting it on the molding as with the panels of a dropped ceiling (*page 109, Step 5*).

124

Hides, Holes and Blinds of the Past

There are as many tales of old houses containing secret passages and hiding places as there are accounts of places where George Washington slept. Some custodians of historic houses, reluctant to spoil a good story, perpetuate the legends—every bricked-up tunnel and concealed doorway hides a secret.

In truth, there is not much documentation to support most such claims. The hideaways, called hides, and the disguised doorways, called blind doorways or, simply, blinds, were usually built for rather practical reasons—to provide storage, for example, or to maintain architectural symmetry. The numerous "escape" tunnels cited by guides to historic houses may be, more accurately, sewers or water conduits that were left to run dry when more sophisticated plumbing was installed.

Of course, throughout history and around the world there have been true hides and blinds whose purposes have been documented. England is dotted with "priest holes," hideaways built in the 16th Century as protection from militant Protestants—and sometimes later used by shadier characters for whom disappearance seemed timely. In the early days of American settlement, hides were built into houses to provide protection from the Indians and to conceal merchandise from the threat of taxation or thievery.

One famous example of a historic hide is the room in which Britain's Charles II took refuge during the civil wars. In 1651, with the army of Oliver Cromwell at his heels, Charles hid in a secret room at Moseley Old Hall in Staffordshire. The King entered the room through an ingenious double hide tucked behind the wall paneling of a bedroom. The first door to the secret room was cut through the bedroom paneling from floor to ceiling. Behind the panel, a trap door in the floor opened into another small chamber below. Here the King could lie, if not in comfort, at least in safety.

In America, the secret of one of the most famous hides has the distinction of having been protected by a celebrated early author. Nathaniel Hawthorne's *House of the Seven Gables,* published in 1851, makes no direct mention of the secret staircase that is one of the most intriguing features of the house, now a popular tourist attraction in Salem, Massachusetts. Built around a chimney that rises between rooms, and entered through concealed doors latched and hinged on the stairway side, the secret staircase is thought to have been added to the house in 1692 when the notorious witchcraft scare swept through Salem. The theory is that the family of the owner, John Turner II, would have hidden on the staircase, at least temporarily, if hysterical neighbors had accused them of consorting with the devil.

In contrast to the drama of hides constructed for security are those that simply camouflage the oddities of architectural design. At Viscaya, the estate of the late James Deering in Miami, Florida, architectural happenstance has kept the existence of some of the rooms from being generally known. Built in the style of an Italian Renaissance villa, with many of its rooms imported intact from Europe, Viscaya is pieced together from many parts. In connecting its rooms, the architects frequently had to cut doorways in unlikely places and then disguise the doors' existence. One section of bookcase in the library is actually the door into the reception room, and one of the painted panels on a bedroom wall swings on invisible hinges to open onto the balcony.

The demands of architecture—in this case, symmetry—also produced two secret closets in a Beaux-Arts apartment house built in 1916 in Washington, D.C., and currently the headquarters for the National Trust for Historic Preservation. On the ground floor, a central rotunda slices into the rectangular living rooms of two facing apartments, creating four wedges of space.

In one of the apartments, these spaces are used as closets, their existence camouflaged by two towering built-in bookcases, whose lower sections are actually doors *(below)*. The bookcase shelves continue above the top of the door, concealing the break in the bookcase structure, and the decorative molding at the side of the door is mitered to make the joints unnoticeable when the door is closed.

A door disguised as a bookcase. These shelves swing open on blind pivot hinges, revealing a closet in an apartment once occupied by famous hostess Perle Mesta. A small button, hidden in the molding, retracts the latch.

Picture Credits

The sources for the illustrations in this book are shown below. The drawings were created by Jack Arthur, Lazlo Bodrogi, Roger Essley, Charles Forsythe, Dick Lee, John Martinez, Joan S. McGurren and W. F. McWilliam.

Cover: Fil Hunter. 6: Fil Hunter. 8-10: Eduino J. Pereira. 11-17: Frederic F. Bigio from B-C Graphics. 18-22: Eduino J. Pereira. 23-33: John Massey. 34, 35: Frederic F. Bigio from B-C Graphics. 36: Fil Hunter. 39-43: Walter Hilmers Jr. from HJ Commercial Art. 45-47: Elsie Hennig. 49: Eduino J. Pereira. 50-57: Frederic F. Bigio from B-C Graphics. 58-61: Walter Hilmers Jr. from HJ Commercial Art. 62, 63: John Massey. 64: Adisai Hemintranont from Sai Graphis. 65: Courtesy W. F. Norman Corporation. 66: Fil Hunter. 69-75: Ray Skibinski. 76-81: Snowden Associates Inc. 83-93: Frederic F. Bigio from B-C Graphics. 94-101: John Massey. 102: Fil Hunter. 105-113: Frederic F. Bigio from B-C Graphics. 114-121: Walter Hilmers Jr. from HJ Commercial Art. 122-124: Snowden Associates Inc. 125: W. F. McWilliam.

Acknowledgments

The index/glossary for this book was prepared by Louise Hedberg. The editors also wish to thank the following: Marc Alberding, Wheaton, Md.; Anthony N. Tyson Ltd., New York, N.Y.; Kevin Arnold, James A. Hunter, Cub Run Builders, Alexandria, Va.; Jack Baxter, J. E. Builders, Inc., Silver Spring, Md.; John Bennett, Eldorado Stone Corporation, Kirkland, Wash.; Al Boland, W. A. Smoot & Co., Inc., Alexandria, Va.; David Brackett, Gypsum Association, Washington, D.C.; Delia and Rafael Carrillo, New York, N.Y.; Basilio Ciocci, Capitol Restorations, Washington, D.C.; Edward Clark, Panel Brick Manufacturing, Inc., Owensboro, Ky.; Lawrence Dodd, Leonard Muddiman, Dodd Bros., Inc., Falls Church, Va.; Arthur B. Dodge III, Dodge Cork Co., Lancaster, Pa.; Peter C. Eggers, Woden Woods, Denver, Colo.; Mark Elmore, Jimmy Kraft, Fairfax Building Supply, Vienna, Va.; Lawrence R. England Jr., L. R. England & Son, Winchester, Mass.; Federal Bureau of Investigation, Washington, D.C.; Jerry Finkelstein, K-Lux Product Division, K-S-H, Inc., St. Louis, Mo.; Al Fox, Washington, D.C.; Giannetti's Studio, Brentwood, Md.; Robert L. Herman, Dependable Cork Co., Morristown, N.J.; Randolph Hicks Sr., Fredricksburg, Va.; Randolph Hicks Jr., Fredricksburg, Va.; Hytla & Hart, Washington, D.C.; Frank Ireland, Alexandria, Va.; Gurudev Singh Khalsa, Golden Temple Woodworks, Washington, D.C.; Bob Kleinhans, Tile Council of America, Princeton, N.J.; Robert J. Landy, Cork Products Company, Inc., New York, N.Y.; Daniel E. Linaugh Jr., The Brick Shoppe, Inc., Rockville, Md.; John Lopynski, Columbia Mirror and Glass of Georgetown, Inc., Washington, D.C.; Hugh Marshall, Fredricksburg, Va.; Lawrence Martell, Midlothian, Va.; David E. McKee, Expanko Cork Co., West Chester, Pa.; Bob Menaker, Alexandria, Va.; Roy N. Merritt, S. R. Wood, Inc., Clarksville, Ind.; Charles Miller, White Plains, N.Y.; National Concrete Masonry Association, Herndon, Va.; National Park Service, Colonial National Historical Park, Yorktown, Va.; R. Daniel Nicholson Jr., Rockville, Md.; Mary Niver, Williams Panel Brick Manufacturing Co., Inc., Detroit, Mich.; S. W. Palmer-Ball, Palmer Products Corporation, Louisville, Ky.; Frank J. Palumbo, Alexandria, Va.; Robert L. Petersen, Alexandria, Va.; Tim Prentice, Architect, New York, N.Y.; Bob Quinto, W. F. Norman Co., Nevada, Mo.; Jim Ransom, Jim Ransom Tile Contracting, Dickerson, Md.; James Rose, North Hollywood, Calif.; Paul Rudolph, Architect, New York, N.Y.; Hank Ruttura, Barney Brainum—Shanker Steel Co., Glendale, N.Y.; Paul and Kathy Schoellhamer, Washington, D.C.; Harry Simpson, W. A. Smoot & Co., Inc., Alexandria, Va.; Society for the Preservation of New England Antiquities, Boston, Mass.; Bart Spano, P.E., Polysonics, Washington, D.C.; Steve Spooner, Morgan Millwork, Alexandria, Va.; Don Thomas, Ademas Tile, Washington, D.C.; Universal Studios, Special Effects, Universal City, Calif.; Gloria Vanderbilt, New York, N.Y.; Z-Brick Co., Division of VMC Corporation, Woodinville, Wash. The editors are indebted to Jan Cook, Julia Homer, Mark J. LaRocca, Stephen J. Makler and Wendy Murphy, writers, for their assistance with the preparation of this book.

Index/Glossary

Included in this index are definitions of many of the technical terms used in this book. Page references in italics indicate an illustration of the subject mentioned.

Acoustic leaks, plugging, 115, *121*
Acoustic tiles and panels: installing, 104, *105-109. See also* Soundproofing; Tile, ceiling
Adhesive: and brick veneer, 50, 52, 54; and ceramic tile, *36, 38, 40;* and cork, 48; and imitation bricks, *55;* on mirrors, 44, 46; and paneling, 68, *70-71;* on wallboard, 18, *19,* 20, 21
Asbestos, working with, 50

Back-blocking: *method of joining untapered ends of wallboard panels.* In ceiling, 18, *20;* in wall, *21*
Barn boards, 82
Bathtub, laying tiles around, *39-40*
Beams: building simulated, *112;* finishing, *112;* mounting, *113*
Bearing walls: *walls that support second-floor joists or the roof.* In house construction, 8, *9, 10*
Blocking: *horizontal supports that reinforce construction.* Building stud wall, *16;* in raised paneling, *94, 97, 100*
Board paneling. *See* Paneling, solid-wood
Bonding agent, 26
Bookcase, swinging: built to hide recess in wall, *122-123*
Brick, exposing, *56-57*
Brick, imitation, setting, *55*
Brick veneer: attaching panels, 50, *53-54;* cleaning, 50; cutting bricks, *51;* mortaring joints, *52;* patterns, *50*

Ceiling: acoustic tile, 104, *105-107;* applying mortar to, 30; back-blocking, 18, *20;* building with wallboard, 18, *19-20;* enclosing pipes and ducts, *110-111;* false, 122, *124;* lowering, *117;* luminous, 104, *109-110;* and metal-frame dividers, *63;* molding, *81, 107;* preparing, 11; rebuilding, *118;* simulated beams, *112-113;* soundproofing techniques, 103, *114-115, 117-118;* suspended panels, 104, *107-109;* tin, 65
Ceiling medallion, attaching, *34, 35*
Chimney piece: *molding that frames wall space above fireplace.* Attaching to wall, *34, 35;* mitering framing strips, *35*
Composition board, 38
Coping: *method of joining trim in which one piece is cut to follow the profile of the adjoining piece.* Cutting molding, *80, 81, 101*
Cork wall, 37, 48; cutting, *49;* laying out tiles, 48, *49;* mounting sheets, *49;* preparing surface, 48

Door: in metal-stud wall, 62, *63;* sealing cracks around, *121*

Electrical outlet: and ceiling tile, *106;* and cork wall, *49;* cutting hole in wallboard, *19;* in exposed brick wall, 56, *57;* extending box, *17;* and false wall, *15;* and paneling, *74*

Fire codes, 11, 18, 50, 65
Firestops: *staggered 2-by-4s nailed horizontally between studs to slow spread of flames.* In wood-frame construction, 9
Furring: *building out a wall or ceiling with a grid of thin wooden strips to which new surface material is attached.* Base for plywood paneling, *11, 70;* and board paneling, 82, *84, 92;* building a wall, *11, 12-14;* on ceiling, *13, 14;* and ceiling tile, 104, *105-106;* over masonry, *10,* 11; and raised panels, *94, 97, 100;* and tin ceiling, 65

Grout: in ceramic-tile joints, 38, 39, 41, *42-43*
Gypsum: characteristics, 7; lath, 8, 26, 28, *29;* in wallboard, 8, 18. *See also* Wallboard

Hardboard, 67, 69

Insulation: in soundproofing, *114, 115, 116, 117, 118, 120, 121;* and wallboard, 18

Joint compound, 6; amount to buy, 23; sealing joints in wallboard panels, 18, *23-25*
Joint tape, 6; using, 18, *23-25*
Jointer, *52*
Joints: caulking in brick wall, *57;* dowel, *94, 98, 100;* mitered, *59-60;* mortaring in brick veneer, *52;* in raised panels, 94, 97, *98-100;* sealing in wallboard, 18, *23-25;* shiplap, *83;* in solid-wood panels, 67, *83;* tongue-and-groove, 66, 82, *83, 86, 90;* in veneer paneling, 68, *71,* 79
Joists: *horizontal framing members that support ceiling and floor.* Attaching wallboard to, *19-20;* and fluorescent fixtures, 109; in house construction, 8, *9, 10;* and insulation, *118;* locating concealed, *8;* and resilient metal channels, *102, 114,* 115, *118;* and staggered-stud wall, *119;* in suspended ceiling, *108;* and Z channels, *117*
Junction boxes: false wall around, 11; tapping into, *110*

Kerfing: *making saw cuts that enable a board to bend into a curve.* Fitting plywood, 76, *77*

Lath: applying plaster to, 26, 28; gypsum, 8, 26, 28, *29;* metal, 8, *9, 10,* 26, *28;* reinforcing gypsum, *29;* removing, 56; repairs in old lath, 26; wood, 8, *9, 10,* 26, *28. See also* Gypsum; Plaster
Lighting: luminous panel, *109;* mounting fluorescent fixtures behind suspended ceiling, *109-110. See also* Wiring
Luminous ceiling, *109-110*

Masonry: attaching wallboard to, *10;* and brick veneer, 53; building a false wall over, *15;* cleaner, 50; construction, 8, *10;* and furring strips, 11
Mastic: with ceramic tile, *36, 38, 40;* for hanging mirrors, 44, *46, 47*
Metal lath: expanded-metal, 26; repairing small holes in plaster, 26, *28;* woven-wire, 26
Metal-stud wall, *62-64,* 117
Mirrored walls, 37; beveled panels, *46;* hardware, 44, 46, *47;* large panels, *47;* mirror tiles, 44, *45*
Mitering: diagonal board panels, 82; double-angle cuts, *89;* joints, in wooden divider frame, *59-60;* molding, *96;* panel molding, *80,* 81; plaster molding, *35;* raised panels, *98;* in solid-wood paneling, 87, *89, 90, 91*
Moisture barrier, on masonry wall, 11
Molding: cap, *81, 101;* ceiling, *81, 107, 124;* chimney piece, *34, 35;* in Georgian paneling, *94, 100;* mitered, in frame-on-plywood panels, *96;* panel, 79, *80-81;* plaster, mitering, *35;* removing, *12;* in wainscoting, *81, 101*
Mortar: applying base, *30-31;* applying finish, *31-32;* joints in brick veneer, 50, *51, 52;* mixing, 26, *27;* mixing base, *29;* mixing finish, *31;* patching joints in brick, 56, *57*
Muriatic acid: *diluted hydrochloric acid used as wash for masonry.* Washing brick walls with, 56, *57*

127